Touch and Go Joe

of related interest

The ACT Workbook for Teens with OCD
Unhook Yourself and Live Life to the Full
Patricia Zurita Ona Psy.D.
Illustrated by Louise Gardner
Foreword by Stuart Ralph
ISBN 978 1 78775 083 8
eISBN 978 1 78775 084 5

Obsessive Compulsive Disorder Diary
A Self-Help Diary with CBT Activities to Challenge Your OCD
Charlotte Dennis
Foreword by Dr. Amita Jassi and Dr. Zoe Kindynis
ISBN 978 1 78775 053 1
eISBN 978 1 78775 054 8

Stand Up to OCD!
A CBT Self-Help Guide and Workbook for Teens
Kelly Wood and Douglas Fletcher
ISBN 978 1 78592 835 2
eISBN 978 1 78450 973 6

Can I tell you about OCD?
A guide for friends, family and professionals
Dr. Amita Jassi
Illustrated by Sarah Hull
ISBN 978 1 84905 381 5
eISBN 978 0 85700 736 0

Breaking Free From OCD
A CBT Guide for Young People and Their Families
Jo Derisley, Isobel Heyman, Sarah Robinson and Cynthia Turner
ISBN 978 1 84310 574 9
eISBN 978 1 84642 799 2

Touch and Go Joe

Updated Edition

A Teen's Experience of OCD

Joe Wells

Forewords by Dr Amita Jassi and Dr Isobel Heyman
Illustrations by Richy K. Chandler

Jessica Kingsley Publishers
London and Philadelphia

First edition published in Great Britain in 2006 by Jessica Kingsley Publishers
This edition published in Great Britain in 2021 by Jessica Kingsley Publishers
An Hachette Company

1

A CIP catalogue record for this title is available from the
British Library and the Library of Congress

ISBN 978 1 78775 777 6
eISBN 978 1 78775 778 3

Printed and bound in Great Britain by CPI Group

Jessica Kingsley Publishers' policy is to use papers that are natural,
renewable and recyclable products and made from wood grown in
sustainable forests. The logging and manufacturing processes are expected
to conform to the environmental regulations of the country of origin.

Jessica Kingsley Publishers
Carmelite House
50 Victoria Embankment
London EC4Y 0DZ

www.jkp.com

Contents

For Mum

Foreword by Dr Isobel Heyman

I feel as if I have been waiting for this book. Children and teenagers with Obsessive Compulsive Disorder (OCD) have been asking for this book for years. 'You are not alone' is a message young people with OCD most need to hear. Parents, doctors, therapists may say this, but a teenager with OCD will really believe it when they hear it from another teenager with OCD. Joe Wells has written his own very personal account of his struggle with, and recovery from, OCD but incorporates all of the important messages for any young person coping with this illness.

A teenager reading this book, who feels they are the only one dealing with unwelcome, distressing, repetitive thoughts (obsessions) and annoying, time-consuming, repetitive behaviours (compulsions), will learn that these are the characteristic symptoms of OCD. They will also learn, from Joe's account, how OCD can creep up on you, symptoms gradually appearing over months or years. The child with OCD often feels confused, ashamed and secretive, so even close family members may take a while to be aware of the problem, as in Joe's case. A book like this may be just what a young person with OCD needs, to feel able to confide in someone, and begin to get the help they need to recover.

Especially helpful is Joe's account of how OCD symptoms

need not include the familiar rituals of handwashing, or checking, but can include more hidden, but equally distressing, rituals such as counting, or repeating. Other aspects of OCD – intrusive religious, sexual or aggressive thoughts – are often highly distressing to a teenager, yet all are identified as being well-recognized symptoms of OCD. Any teenager reading this section will feel hugely relieved to know that these thoughts are common in OCD, and not some strange manifestation of their own condition.

Joe emphasizes that OCD is not just annoying, it can interfere with many of the pleasurable aspects of life. He explains how it affected his enjoyment of holidays or ability to see his friends, themes familiar to most teenagers with OCD. One of the aims of this book is to help increase awareness and recognition of OCD. Joe gives a moving account of the frustrations he and his family experienced trying to get the correct diagnosis. Perhaps if such a book had existed when Joe first needed to see a doctor, the symptoms of OCD would have been recognized earlier! This book will be a valuable resource for young people with OCD and their families, as well as teachers and other people who work closely with children. Health professionals, even those familiar with OCD, will be enlightened and moved by this personal account.

Joe's account, whilst highlighting some of the fear, exasperation and distress he experienced, also emphasizes how recovery is possible. There are clear accounts of the effective treatments. Talking therapies are often perceived as mysterious and secret, but Joe opens up the therapy room and explains just how practical and sensible good Cognitive Behavioural Therapy should be. He also dispels many of the myths and worries associated with medication for OCD, describing how drugs used carefully, with monitoring, can really help the recovery process for some people.

Perhaps most importantly, Joe emphasizes that OCD should

never be allowed to take over. Anybody with OCD is still themselves, and even whilst in the process of recovery, it is important to 'get on with life'. So for Joe it is certainly no longer Touch and Go...it is Go Joe Go!...

...and that is his message for everyone coping with OCD.

Dr Isobel Heyman
Consultant Psychiatrist
National & Specialist Service for Young People
with OCD, Maudsley Hospital, London

Foreword by Dr Amita Jassi

At the age of 16, Joe Wells took the brave decision to write this book as a young person experiencing OCD. In this updated edition we get a bonus chapter, 16 years on, in which Joe looks back at his teen years and gives us an insight into what life looks like now for him as an adult. All these years later, his experiences and the messages weaved into his story have stood the test of time and are still relevant and important for young people today. The key messages being – you are not alone, and you can get better!

Joe takes us on a journey from when he first started to develop OCD symptoms at the age of nine, through the evolution of his OCD manifesting into different types of symptoms, to his eventual diagnosis and recovery. Unfortunately, despite being 16 years on, this story is a familiar one to me, where young people with this common condition often have delays in recognition, diagnosis and effective treatment, especially for the lesser-known obsessions and compulsions. The important message that Joe shares is that even if it feels scary, embarrassing, shameful or all of the above, it is important not to keep OCD a secret. Once you can tell others what is going on, you have a better chance of accessing the support you need.

Joe shares how his OCD manifested in different ways and

evolved over time, which is common. It started with the better-known handwashing rituals, moving onto lesser-known rituals, including mental rituals (saying phrases in his head), tapping, walking in particular ways, blinking, and counting. Joe talks about the obsessions he had, such as contamination worries, fear of God and fear of other people dying. This is just the tip of the iceberg – one thing that has kept me interested in working with OCD since 2006 is that you will always hear about a vast range of obsessions and compulsions; you sometimes even hear things you may not have heard about before! OCD can pick on any thought (that we all get from time to time) and make it intrusive, repetitive and distressing. This is true of compulsions too – we all have habits that we have to do – but OCD can take it to the extreme and make you feel you absolutely must do them. As Joe says, we all have intrusive thoughts and annoying habits, but with OCD they cause distress and interfere in people's lives. It is important to remember that regardless of the type of OCD you have, it works in the same way and the treatment is the same.

Joe speaks openly about his experience of the two evidence-based treatments for OCD: Cognitive Behavioural Therapy (CBT) and medication, namely selective serotonin re-uptake inhibitors (SSRIs). Joe talks about how in his CBT he challenged thoughts and completed experiments to see if what OCD was saying would come true. Another important part is Exposure and Response Prevention (ERP) where you face OCD triggers, resist doing what OCD wants you to do (compulsions, avoidance or seeking reassurance) and tolerate the anxiety, which eventually comes down. You can learn something about whether OCD is telling the truth or not, but sometimes OCD can plant thoughts and ideas that are hard to prove such as going to hell or something bad happening in the future, so it is about tolerating the anxiety and uncertainty. The more you do ERP, starting with easier compulsions and moving onto harder ones, the easier it gets and eventually OCD starts to back off! Joe reveals how CBT wasn't easy, which many will relate to, but it did help.

Joe talks about the impact OCD had on his family, social life, confidence and mood. What he highlights is it is really difficult for families to know what is going on at first and what to do for the best, which is completely understandable. It is important parents know that it is not their fault or their child's fault that they have OCD. I describe it is an unlucky lottery (although you have more chance of getting OCD than winning the lottery!) We do not know the cause, but we know treatment works and that is the important thing to remember. Another important message to take away from this book is that OCD is not you – it is not part of your personality, it is not your identity, it is something you suffer from. You are still you!

Joe shares his story with warmth, courage, honesty and humour to give insight into what he experienced. This makes him relatable to young people and means his story will resonate with many people with OCD. Just like the original edition, this book will help so many young people out there with this common condition.

Dr Amita Jassi
Consultant Clinical Psychologist
National and Specialist OCD, BDD and Related Disorders Clinic
for Young People, South London and Maudsley NHS Trust

Acknowledgements

Thanks to my family who were a massive help to me throughout the course of OCD and extra thanks to my mum, without whom I could never have got this book in print: thank you for nagging me to keep on writing and for negotiating the more boring aspects of getting a book published. To Alison Wallis who also helped me through OCD. To my rock and roll idols whose music will always keep my spirits high. To Stephen Jones for taking the time to read my proposal and helping me to get this book through to publication. To Sally Flynn for proofreading at short notice. To all my friends, too many to name, but you know who you are: I know I can always rely on you for help and support. Thank you to Jake Young who proofread the extra chapter for the new edition. And finally to OCD: the joke's on you, as in the end you only made me stronger.

I would also like to thank everyone who gave their permission in order for the quotes to be used in this book.

Extract from *Owl Babies* written by Martin Waddell and illustrated by Patrick Benson. Text © 1992 Martin Waddell. Reproduced by permission of Walker Books Ltd, London.

What's This Book About?

This book is about OCD or Obsessive Compulsive Disorder. Not much has been written about it before and that which has is full of confusing medical jargon which you would need a PhD in psychology to understand. This book however has had the jargon trimmed off; you don't need it really. I am writing this book because I have OCD and I want to tell you what it's like, so that I hope for other people it won't be quite the same; you can learn from my mistakes instead of making your own.

Chapter 1

Worrying

'Suppose she got lost,' said Sarah. 'Or a fox got her,' said Percy. 'I want my mummy,' said Bill.

— MARTIN WADDELL, OWL BABIES

Hi, my name's Joe, just Joe, not Joseph, although I'm always getting called Joseph. I'm 16 now and I live in the south of England. I come from a fairly ordinary and functioning family and have good friends who I see regularly. I'm quite a confident person (well, now I am, I never used to be) and I love music. I'm currently looking for more space to store my hundreds of CDs, from Aphex Twin to Frank Zappa. I also like art and I'm hoping to go to the Saatchi Gallery in London with my friends after my GCSEs. Oh, and until recently I have had OCD.

But don't worry, I'm very safe and there's no cause for alarm. OCD isn't like the mental illness that you see in horror films. I don't run a creepy motel, I've never scrawled 'RED RUM' on my bedroom wall, and I would never be rude about my vicar's mother. I'm actually just an ordinary guy. OCD is Obsessive *Compulsive* Disorder, so it only affects the things that you do, not the way that you are or the way that you feel (except for the fact that it can stress you out at times). Basically OCD makes you over-concerned with things that other people might see as trivial or perhaps wouldn't have thought about at all, like turning off the oven or making sure that your hands are clean.

OCD is something which I developed from a young age and at first it meant that I was overly concerned about cleanliness, but then I moved on to some slightly more obscure concerns. Like I said, I'm very safe and OCD sticks out from the stereotype of mental illness like a sore thumb. OCD is a completely unique illness; it cannot easily be compared to other mental illnesses. In fact we all have some characteristics of OCD. Anyone who has ever checked twice if they've left their oven on, or anyone who has ever worried about the sell-by date of that yoghurt they just ate, is experiencing similar symptoms to someone with OCD. OCD is excessive worrying (see Appendix 1 for the expanded definition of OCD). However, it is only considered OCD when it has started to disrupt your life. I began to develop OCD around the age of nine. As a normal child going to an ordinary school this was very hard for me. OCD is also a completely irrational disorder, especially as I was a nine-year-old with nothing much to worry about except my next spelling test. My mind became fixed on worrying thoughts and instead of having a good time with my friends I was often sat on my own hoping that the solvents in the wallpaper paste wouldn't be the end of me.

Obsessive Compulsive Disorder does exactly what it says on the tin: it gives you obsessive thoughts, compelling you to do irrational things. At this time these obsessive thoughts were the fear of contamination or as I, the nine-year-old child, would say, 'poisoning'. However, later on, I developed even more irrational compulsions.

OCD affects up to two per cent of the population (according to OCD-UK) including the actor Leonardo DiCaprio, the pop star Niall Horan and probably many other people who are unwilling to admit it. Two in 100 may not seem like a lot but if these statistics are true it would mean that in my school year of 300 it's likely that five other children were affected by it, and in my school of 1500, 30 people were affected. That's a whole minibus full of people worrying throughout the day.

The exact process of OCD is very hard to explain to someone who has never experienced it. When I try to explain it to people, their reaction, although sympathetic, is often similar to my reaction when arachnophobes try to explain to me why they do not like spiders, but here goes: it is a sort of self-fulfilling prophecy, where my mind will try to not worry about something and therefore does worry about it. A lot. The best example in an 'ordinary' person's life that I can give you is this:

Do not think about tomatoes; try really hard to get all thoughts of bright red tomatoes out of your head. Why would one want to think about tomatoes anyway? Ignore the tomatoes and remove them from your mind.

Whilst reading that sentence I know that the one thing that you were probably thinking about the most was tomatoes. For most people this is not a problem. As long as no one is talking directly about the thing that they do not want to think about, they go on with their normal lives. However, for someone with OCD this is not the case. The thoughts would stay with them all day. This plague of thoughts is another thing that is hard to explain to an 'ordinary' person, but the most similar phenomenon that I can think of is having a song stuck in your head. We've all had times at school, college or work when we are trying to mind our own business, but can't stop humming Britney Spears' 'Oops I Did It Again'.

It's the same feeling of unwanted thoughts pestering their way into your everyday thoughts. But they weren't thoughts of tomatoes. In fact, unwanted tomato-related thoughts aren't to my knowledge an existing form of OCD. People can have thoughts that something might infect them, because they have failed to avoid infection, or that they have to fulfil ridiculous rituals of touching things a certain amount of times, or walking with certain steps. I would get a thought in my mind, a worry, and that thought would not go away. The thought would plague me all day long. It kept getting at me, all day long; it was unbearable. I COULD NOT TAKE IT! Eventually, after much futile objection, I allowed the thought to overpower me and force me to do whatever action it was asking me to do. It was like a young child whining and whining until it got its own way, until the parent screams, 'FINE, YOU CAN LEAVE YOUR VEGETABLES, BUT JUST THIS ONCE!', 'FINE I'LL BUY YOU THAT TOY, BUT JUST THIS ONCE!' or 'FINE, YOU CAN STAY UP A BIT PAST YOUR BEDTIME, BUT JUST THIS ONCE!'. But any good parent knows that the more you keep saying 'just this once', 'just this once' to a child the harder it gets to refuse their requests. I kept saying 'just this once', 'just this once' to OCD and in the end it took a tight grip around me and could never be told 'no'. It was like a spoilt little brat that would always get its own way. The system was simple: Thoughts = Actions.

No questions, no arguments. It was as though these thoughts combined with my OCD were totalitarian dictators: what they say goes and I'd have no say in it whatsoever. I was a slave to these thoughts and actions – thoughts and actions which have varied as I have grown up. My first worries are detailed in the next chapter.

SUMMARY

» Everybody has some irrational obsessions like checking twice that they've locked the door, or being a bit fussy with sell-by dates, but it's when these things get in the way of your normal life and are distressing for you that you might have OCD.

» OCD is very hard to explain to people who don't have OCD.

» OCD can gain power over you. When you try not to think about your obsession you can't take your mind off it.

» OCD is not rare; in fact up to two per cent of the population are affected by it in some way.

Chapter 2

Poisoning of the Mind

If swallowed, seek medical advice immediately and show this container or label. After contact with skin, wash immediately with plenty of water.

– SAFETY PRECAUTIONS ON DOMESTOS THICKEST EVER BLEACH

For me it was a frightening thought that I could be harmed by something without realizing it: a small bacterium, the fumes of a car exhaust, or even the solvents in a recently painted room. I was constantly obsessing that there was something that would 'poison' me and the only way that I felt I could relax and believe that I would live was to receive reassurance from my parents that I would be OK. This was a real problem at school when my parents were not there to help me. In order to avoid any chance of contamination I decided that it would be safer to wash my hands around ten times a day and not to touch anything that may not be safe, such as pen ink, correction fluid or even the door handles.

This obsession was not helped at all by our local policewoman, who once a month would come round our school to give us long lectures on the dangers of drugs. One thing she seemed to focus on – which now seems strange to me, as it is something that I have never come into contact with – was 'solvent abuse'. She would

tell us these horrific stories of how people had sniffed their deodorant cans and then died on the spot. The police thought that
this was warning us against drug abuse, but actually it pushed me
further into my paranoia about poisoning. Now I had evidence
given to me, from a reliable source, that everyday objects could
have drastic health implications. Solvents are used in the ink of
most commercial printing; they are in the paint on the walls, the
deodorant you wear, and the varnish on most wooden objects.
My house was truly a frightening place.

To protect myself from these household poisons I would cover my
hand with the end of my sleeve if I had to touch a contaminated
object. This acted as a barrier to prevent the germs entering my
body. Although this acted as a temporary solution I now realize
that it was unconstructive. Another self-fulfilling prophecy was
that the more I worried about my impending death, the more
sick I would feel. This in turn confirmed that I was in fact going

to die, and therefore this knowledge made me feel even more sick. This spiral of fear of sickness and actual sickness would just deteriorate until I had my fears invalidated by an adult.

This obsession also caused me problems at school and there was even an incident where I found myself so worried in a lesson that I was unable to work. We were told to draw what we thought the sound waves of a song looked like. Earlier another child had given me something that I believed to be contaminated. I then became so obsessed that I was unable to move my hand to work. My teacher asked me why I wasn't working and I replied vaguely that I felt really bad, so I was sent to the sick bay where I tried to explain to the nurse what my problem was, but she did not understand. She phoned my mum who calmed me down over the phone so I was able to go back to class.

The constant hand washing often made my hands sore and after I had washed my hands at school I would have to nudge the tap off with my wrist, so I did not touch the tap or anything else that other people may have touched with dirty hands.

This aspect of my OCD was a particularly noticeable feature especially as at age nine, when my friends had a general disregard for personal hygiene, I would be washing my hands like Lady Macbeth.

Some people might assume that the reason I became like this at a young age was because of my parents: children emulate their parents so my parents must have been hygiene freaks. No, not at all. In my early childhood I was always out in the back garden playing amongst the dirt, or out on the beach making sandcastles, or making things with glue and paint and old cardboard boxes. So that's one myth that can be put out with the rubbish. But there's plenty more to come.

SUMMARY

» Some people who have OCD become obsessed with avoiding infection and germs (known as 'fear of contamination').

» Of course you should keep yourself clean, and try to stay healthy, but you must always be sensible about what precautions you take to avoid germs.

» If you know that you have these worries try to take 'health warnings' with a pinch of salt. Stay calm.

» If half your brain says 'Come on, you don't need to keep washing your hands', listen to that half, not the half saying, 'You had better wash your hands again because you touched the door handle on the way out of the bathroom.'

» Germs are inescapable, so apart from taking the precautions that everyone else does, e.g. washing your hands after you go to the loo, don't worry about them.

Chapter 3

Only Human

One day Arthur came home from school. He looked even more worried than usual.

– JOAN STIMSON, WORRIED ARTHUR

Name:	Joe Wells
Age:	16
Height:	OCD
Eye colour:	OCD
Hair:	OCD
Address:	The world of prejudgement and stereotypes
Favourite song:	OCD
Favourite book:	OCD
Favourite film:	OCD
Favourite painting:	OCD
Pet hate:	OCD
Favourite activity:	OCD
Description:	Is very OCD but does have tendencies of OCD. Joe is often found OCD. But will

sometimes venture OCD at the weekends or on a Friday night. Sometimes likes to visit the OCD or just to OCD with friends.

Or is it more like this?

Name:	Joe Wells
Age:	16
Height:	Taller than my mum but not quite as tall as my dad
Eye colour:	Blue/green
Hair:	Thick, brown and irritatingly curly
Address:	The real world
Favourite song:	'There is a Light That Never Goes Out' by The Smiths
Favourite book:	*Thus Spoke Zarathustra* by Friedrich Nietzsche
Favourite film:	*The Wicker Man*
Favourite painting:	'The Scream' by Edvard Munch
Pet hate:	PE teachers
Favourite activity:	Writing, drawing, listening to music
Description:	Is very friendly but does have tendencies of arrogance. Joe is often found at home. But will sometimes venture down town at the weekends or on a Friday night. Sometimes likes to visit the cinema or just to chat with friends.

Something that a lot of people find difficult to understand is that OCD isn't a hobby or a personality trait; it doesn't take away from me being me, nor does it add to me. I am a person, no more and no less than every other person. And all people have one thing in common: vulnerability.

If aliens were testing the physical ability of creatures on earth, humans would get a very low score. They can't run that fast; even the six-foot tall muscly ones in the Olympics have nothing on a cheetah. Human skin is easily pierced and the vital organs are protected only by a rib-cage of bones, nothing like the strong exoskeleton of a crab. Humans have only one stomach, unlike the standard four of a cow, and can't even eat grass. We are very vulnerable creatures. Our bodies are susceptible to disease and where does it get in? Usually the mouth.

When I was about ten years old, I used to find this a very disturbing thought. When I ate food, there was no sure way of telling what was in it. Germs are so small that they are invisible to the naked eye. So how could I have been able to tell that the packet of Cheddars that I was eating for lunch did not have some deadly disease on it?

My OCD told me (as a twisted form of logic, rather than a voice in my head) that food straight out of a packet was OK because, of course, the factories where the food is made are cleaned, especially for making food safe. However, how could I be sure that this was true for the surface that I was eating off?

For example, if I dropped one of my crisps onto the collapsible table which we would eat our lunch off, how could I be sure that it was completely clean? How could I trust that the cleaning agents that were used when wiping the tables didn't have solvents in them?

Still now I acknowledge the supreme physical inferiority of the human race to the elements. Yet it was the overwhelming paranoia of this which was one of the most damaging elements of my OCD. My advice to anyone experiencing these feelings is therefore to lie back and relax and try not to think about it too much. Ignorance is bliss and, in small doses, ignorance can be good for you. It sounds easier than it is, but just try not to give in. You will find that after you have been absolutely wetting yourself with worry for a while, you will gradually cool off and eventually be calm again and the odds are that you won't see an early grave just because you accidentally breathed in whilst spraying yourself with deodorant.

It was around this time – when I was 10- or 11-ish and struggling with these poison worries – that my family decided to move from our modest semi-detached house, in the small village of Cowplain, to a slightly larger, detached house in a nearby village, Lovedean. It was not a drastic move, in fact it was only a couple of miles down the road, but from a young age I had not liked leaving places in the fear that I might leave something behind. It was an unnatural fear of leaving something intangible behind me that was beginning to encroach on my life (probably brought on by teachings about souls and spirits that I received at my Sunday school). Later this would germinate into other rituals but at the time it merely inflamed my fear of poisoning.

My bathroom was where the fears formed a focus with cans of deodorant, bleach and a small collection of shells which my OCD had taken a particular dislike to. This had been after seeing a similar shell in a book of dangerous and poisonous creatures. The fear of poisoning was now far beyond rational. I was given a book of puzzles in which there was a maze with certain pathways blocked by 'radioactive waste'. I was a big fan of this puzzle book series, as my mum worked to promote them at the time, but I could not even bear to touch the book. This I knew was irrational.

Why would the poison have been anywhere near it? It's only a picture. Why would a picture of this threatening thing bother me? A picture of a shark or a lion wouldn't bother me, although I wouldn't much like to be in the presence of such an animal. Even when I bought a CD that had a B-side with the word 'toxic' in the title, I felt sure that it could do me harm, and I was not able to listen to it. When I put on the CD, I would have to programme it out with the memory function on the CD player.

The big day of our move came, and I was whisked off to school before I had time to think. When I was picked up to go home I was taken to my new house. It was more or less completely empty. In my room there was nothing but a mattress that would be there temporarily until my new bed arrived. Living in an empty room in a house which didn't feel my own was an unnerving experience to say the least. My OCD got even worse.

Being 11, I spent a large amount of my waking hours at primary school. The school days for someone with OCD, however, are very different to what someone without OCD might expect. My OCD was most visible at lunch time. We would queue up behind laminated signs indicating our year and whether we were to have a packed lunch or pay for hot food. We would be led past the toilets and into the dining room. I would usually have to go into the toilets to wash my hands one more time. So as not to draw attention to this fact, I would drop off from friends and go in to wash my hands on my own. This meant I'd go into the canteen late, usually with my packed lunch, and sit on the end of the tables. That was one of many ways that having OCD meant that I did not have that many friends in primary school. It was not because people did not like me, but that I did not want to go round to friends' houses, or down the park, because I thought it was likely that I would either be seen protecting myself from poison, or I would potentially become contaminated with poison and not have anyone to comfort me.

One thing that OCD is very good at is making you feel very small. The fact that I couldn't even enter a recently painted room was not going to make me feel 'all powerful'. Even after OCD has been largely brought under control, a lack of confidence can still linger on for a long time. I now dread having to go to interviews for jobs. When you have OCD you are at risk of being seen carrying out your rituals whenever people are looking at you, so making eye contact has been hard for me. Although when writing this book it is hard to tell which parts of me are due to OCD and which are parts of my personality I definitely feel that my lack of confidence now is because of my OCD. Not being confident is a hard trait to cope with and people may feel that you are inferior because you are finding it hard to talk to them. I would never ask someone else if they fancied meeting up at the weekend, so they would rarely ask me. Later in my OCD's life I gave up on futile attempts to fit in and stayed at home most weekends, maybe going shopping with my parents, which is always good fun.

I started listening to rock music, my favourite singer being Marilyn Manson, who sung about not fitting in and being isolated in society. You can see why this appealed to me. I read books by authors like Friedrich Nietzsche, who revealed to me that popularity was very much an illusion. I liked the way that these people who were isolated took that feeling that I hated and turned it into something artistic and this was helpful to me at this time. I started drawing and writing, which is very helpful if you enjoy it. I liked especially to write light-hearted essays and poems about the things that I came into contact with. The few people that I did talk to at school liked these, which helped me become more popular. A favourite was the following.

HOW PHILOSOPHY RENDERED TRIGONOMETRY IRRELEVANT

'If man were wise he would gauge the true worth of anything by its usefulness and appropriateness to his life.' Michel de Montaigne, one of the most famous philosophers ever, made the controversial move to stand up against the uselessness of the education system of his time. Yet still little has changed. Irrelevant information is still fed to us in order to pass tests of irrelevant knowledge. In a system of education which should be preparing you for work, we are not taught how to keep good relationships with colleagues or how to cope when your computer crashes. We are taught to learn how to find the remaining sides in a right-angled triangle. But before I go off on negativity to show that I can give a balanced argument, here is a list of situations and occupations which require a strong knowledge of trigonometry:
Situations:

1. If you get abducted by aliens and they promise not to take you back to their home planet if you teach them the ways of trigonometry.
2. If you get stranded on a desert island with nothing but a protractor, a ruler and a calculator and need to keep yourself sane.
3. If you go on *Mastermind and* get asked a question on trigonometry.

Occupations:

1. Triangleologist.
2. Maths teacher.

The reason now that I feel it is especially important that we demolish the teaching of trigonometry is the vast range of computers and radars that we in the twenty-first century are blessed with. If we are in a job where we need to know how tall something is or how far away it is, when we cannot measure it with a tape measure then we are given a radar, or one of those cool wheels that the PE department hide from us. Are we really supposed to believe that RAF pilots carry a pen, paper and a protractor in their planes in order to tell how far away other planes are? By the time they've 'carried the two' it might be too late to avoid that head-on collision. They merely look on their radar.

My final argument which should put any traces of this evil practice into its grave is the fact that it is of course very un-Christian to indulge in this activity. May I remind you of the great sacrifice of Jesus Christ to wipe away our sins, and I'm sure that if he hadn't been busy performing miracles and the likes, he would have got round to 'cos' and 'tan'.

Concluding on a personal level: being from a generation who couldn't understand why disabled parking spaces were bigger than normal parking spaces, I feel that less effort should be put into teaching us to be smart and more effort should be put into making us less stupid.

Joe Wells

People thought that this essay and others were funny and for that I felt they respected me more. But still, having OCD it was hard for me to make friends and it wasn't until I was in Year 9 that I began to make strong friendships. It was weird, people starting to accept me, because for so many years I felt I had been universally hated at school. I can remember a party in Year 7 where the whole class were invited, even those whom I saw as 'different' – everyone except for me. But as people began to accept me it was like a weight being lifted off my back. The irony is that all the years that I had tried to fit in, I had failed to do so. But when I just stood back and let people take me or leave me for who I was, people accepted me more.

SUMMARY

» Even if you do have OCD, you are still a person with a name, along with likes, dislikes, talents, shortcomings, etc. Nothing can take that from you.

» OCD can be triggered or made worse by stressful situations, like moving house, starting a new school, or a friend or family member dying.

» You can find something (legal) which you find calming, like a certain type of book, music or art that you like, and exploit its calming effect to its full potential.

» Doing something artistic also helps to calm you down when OCD is strong.

Chapter 4

Guilty Mind

'Jesus is lord.' Believe in your heart that God raised him from the dead, then you will be saved.

- ROMANS 10:9

I was brought up in a family of Christian values and this meant that I would go to church every now and then. At my church, to encourage young people to go, they would have youth groups to help us to 'know' Jesus. At that age I was not able to go out on my own so I would go to these groups to meet up with friends; it seemed like a good idea. At one of these groups that I attended, I would be taught all about the devil, death and the punishment for sin. The punishment for sin, they told me, was death. At the age of around ten, I could not grasp the idea of eternal life after death, or spiritual deadness. All that I could understand from what they told me was that if I sin then I will die. They also told me all about sin. Sin was, for example, thinking evil thoughts about false idols. The tomato theory therefore meant that because I knew that I should not think about false idols, my mind then became full of these thoughts that I was told would kill me.

One might think that this is out of context as Christians believe in a loving God, but even the bible advises us to 'Fear the lord, my son'. 'God' also flooded the world, sent ten plagues to the people of Egypt and even killed his own son! So he's not someone that you would want to get on the wrong side of. My fear of God grew into another part of my OCD. It was seeming that just at a time when I could get over one aspect of my OCD, it was being replaced by another, even more horrific than the last. Of course, I have not mentioned yet that it was not until much later that my disorder would be recognized as 'obsessive compulsive'. So although my fear of poisoning would have appeared strange to my parents, my new fear of God would be even stranger, so I did not tell them. Another exciting part of the Christian message was the idea that if I believed in Jesus as my Saviour then I would be saved from damnation. And vice versa: if I did not accept Jesus as my Saviour, I was going to burn in hell. It was in response to this belief that I would feel the need to recite in my head, 'I do believe in God and I do accept him in my life' – and then the same for Jesus.

This behaviour was very dangerous as it took all my concentration to keep my mind focused on reciting these things. I could not concentrate on what I was doing and this was something which got worse and more noticeable as time went on. Looking back I am confused. Why weren't there any checks to make sure that these church groups weren't saying anything that could be damaging to potentially vulnerable children like myself? I know from humorous anecdotes of 'political correctness gone mad', and from my mum, who works with children, that the Government keeps tough checks in the health service to ensure that children are safe from things being said that might harm them. Also in schools teachers keep a watchful eye over the content of lessons. However, in churches I think that this isn't the case! I have seen several incidents where things have been said in a church which could be seen as racist, homophobic or distasteful. I'm not attacking the Christian church but I am asking people to be aware of comments that could do harm to the vulnerable – particularly when explaining religious ideas to children.

So there I was, reciting prayers over and over like an anxious monk. This was one of the main times when I started to lose touch with the outside world. I had retracted into my head and wasn't really living the life that I wanted. This was when I entered the dark forest of OCD from which it was going to be a long and difficult escape.

When I was 15 I returned to one of the groups that I talked about earlier, Youth Alpha. My OCD is much more under control now yet I was reminded at this group of the dangers that Christian or any other form of religious extremism could present to people with OCD or anyone prone to being frightened by this kind of activity. After the usual warm-up game, all the group (aged 10 to 16 years old) were brought down into the main church where we were informed that we were going to have the 'Holy Spirit' put into us. They then told us that the supreme power of the Holy Spirit might make us do unusual things – for example, we might feel a weakness in our legs or we might start crying or even speaking in tongues. This all seemed particularly strange to me, half thinking that my head was going to spin round like that bit in *The Exorcist*. However, to a child of 10 years old, as some of the children there were, who could potentially have OCD, I could imagine that this would have been a terrifying image which would not help their obsessive thoughts.

Another thing which was combined with this fear of God and OCD-induced lack of confidence was my fear of authority at school. I went to a Catholic school with a strict authoritarian regime. The teachers who dealt with discipline at my school would often seem to be the harsh and dauntingly emotionless ones. One teacher I remember, even on the last day when everybody was having cake on the sunken lawn, stood atop a three-foot-high wall so as to check that people weren't having too much fun. She wore layers of make-up and had cold eyes like a shark and would never speak unless she had something spiteful to say. Although most of the teachers at my school were good and decent people the omnipresent threat of discipline was, I believe, on everybody's mind, even if just a little bit.

One tool which the school would use, following the outlawing of beating, was what they called 'the inclusions room'. A stupid title really to give to a room where people go to be *excluded* from their class. Anyway, every now and then, a senior member of staff, often the shark-eyed woman, would enter a class uninvited and ask for a pupil go with them. But what happened to them? Would they come back? Would the meat pies from the canteen taste funny the next day? It turns out that the inclusions room was just a room beside the library where people were detained for up to eight hours, sometimes staying until half past five in the afternoon. There they would do lines, essays, whatever the subject teacher thought would best make them conform to the school ethos. At my school there was never any questioning of what the staff said. Our school code of conduct describes cooperation as 'doing what you are asked to do without question or argument'! I saw people getting escorted out of class on a weekly basis and was worried that one day they would come for me. My parents realized that I was getting anxious about school and one day came in with me to have a chat with my then head of year. I thought he was a good bloke – slightly eccentric, but kind – and he assured me that it was a select few whose visits to the inclusion room were a recurrence and that it was only for severe violations of the school rules. This meeting comforted me and I came to the conclusion that it's helpful to talk to school staff if you feel comfortable doing so. It was this same teacher who later was the first person, apart from a family member or a doctor, who I spoke to about having OCD.

SUMMARY

» The church and religion in general can be a challenge to someone with OCD – the things to remember are to always think for yourself and be sensible.
» Don't worry about what you do in your head. In this world it's what you do and say and how you behave that matters, not what thoughts you have.
» It's helpful to question everything that you are told, even things that you tell yourself.

Chapter 5

Am I Going Mad?

Do you hear voices?

– A LOCUM GP, AFTERNOON PRACTICE

My thoughts then moved on to something less religious yet even harder to cope with: the need to try to counter bad thoughts which could have bad outcomes in the real world. For example, my OCD told me that I should not think in my head 'I want "so and so" to die' and that if I did have this thought, I needed to cancel it out by thinking the opposite. To complicate things further, it also told me that if I was closer to the person concerned then my thoughts would have more effect so I would lean my head towards the person in my thought in order to recite the correct one. For example, if I accidentally had the thought that I wanted my mum to die then I would lean my head slightly towards her and recite in my head that I didn't want her to die.

This was hard enough but real problems came when I did not know where the person was so I would have to lean my head in four opposite directions and recite it for each direction. If I messed up I would have to start again! One day a few weeks after our house move, I was in McDonald's with my mum and sister sitting eating our food. The thoughts came into my head that I wanted someone to die (I can't now remember who it was) and I had to counteract those thoughts in each of the four directions. My head was jerking violently back, forth, left and right until my mum saw me making these head movements and told me to stop – people were starting to stare at me because I looked so odd. When I didn't, she pleaded and kept begging me to. I thought that she was making a big deal out of things. I didn't think that anyone could see, and I wouldn't be able to live with myself if anything happened to this person so I thought that it would be worth displeasing my mum as I didn't want to take the risk. The compulsions started to irritate my mum as she saw me not stopping as an act of voluntary defiance, not understanding that for me there was no stopping – I *had* to finish the ritual.

She wasn't shouting as she didn't want to cause a scene in the middle of a fast-food restaurant, yet it was clear that I was in trouble. It was the same feeling that you get when you've been caught doing something that you shouldn't be doing but your parents have friends round and don't want to look bad in front of them: I was going to be in trouble when I got home and it was something that I could not justify. I think she realized eventually that I could not stop and let me continue. In my ignorance I thought 'Well, that's that sorted, I can move my head now' but really I knew that she hadn't forgotten or accepted it but that the subject was going to rear its cringe-inducing head later that evening.

As I expected, later on that night came a rather awkward conversation, which was to be the first time that my parents confronted me about my actions. Both of them together made it impossible for me to talk my way out of anything. My mum asked about what I had been doing in McDonald's and my dad asked about a time a few weeks before where I had been swaying on my way to school (instead of moving my head, I might sway as I walk, to be more left or right). Then, for the first time, I did my best to explain. I was nervous and embarrassed and found it hard to describe the thoughts and therefore I received nothing from my parents except a confused yet concerned look. They felt it appropriate (as most people in that situation would also feel it appropriate) to take me to the GP.

The young doctor who I saw was not my usual doctor, who has a good understanding of mental health, but a young locum GP, a guy who did not appear to know what was wrong with me. I came in, with my mum, extremely nervous of what he might say. I did my best to explain to him what was happening in my mind. After a long explanation (which to be fair I did very badly) the doctor decided to look in my ears and check my breathing. 'You don't understand,' I thought. 'It's in my thoughts.'

He said, 'So do you think it might be more of a psychological thing?'

It was at this point that I felt completely sure that this guy had no idea. 'Yes,' I replied.

'OK,' he said, trying to look as though he knew something about mental health. He leant forward on his chair and asked me a question that I would never forget.

'Do you hear voices?' he asked. He was looking at me like he was trying to work out if I was really a vampire or something and I was doing the same to him.

'What do you mean voices?' I asked.

He replied, 'In your head. Do you hear voices in your head?'

'No, it's not like that,' I explained. 'It's my thoughts, my own thoughts thinking.'

Nothing much came of that visit except a new fear, but this time not one that would be amplified by OCD: people were going to have to know about my thoughts in order to help me, but it was possible that they would not understand what was happening in my head. This fear made me even more determined to keep my thoughts to myself.

I also concluded from this experience that for other people who have OCD but don't recognize it as such, they would be likely to first contact one of three people:

» teacher
» religious leader
» general practitioner.

Unfortunately none of these three people are likely to know much about OCD. This is a big problem; OCD appeared to me to be some kind of scandal. I didn't want to talk about it and neither did other people. And if nobody is talking about something then I cannot find out more about it and therefore can't recover from it.

What is the treatment? Is there treatment? Was I going to have to go to some 'OCD Anonymous' group?

SUMMARY

» OCD is not the experience of 'hearing voices'.

» People won't always understand when someone tries to describe OCD to them. My mistake was not explaining it clearly enough – it's best to be as clear as possible when talking about it.

» Don't expect your GP to know much about OCD. GPs are *general* practitioners but should be able to refer you on to someone who specializes in illnesses like OCD.

» Don't let bad experiences put you off telling people that you have OCD: you are much better off with it out in the open.

Chapter 6

Learning to Count

Being in Year 6, you feel like a big fish in a small pond. Being in Year 7 can feel like being a small fish in a much bigger pond

— MY SECONDARY SCHOOL HEADMASTER

The counting was the final evolution of my OCD. I cannot remember when my counting started. However, although it is the one of the less talked about parts of OCD, I found that it was the hardest to cope with. It reached a pinnacle when I went up to secondary school. Everyone was bigger than me and I was, as my head teacher would say, 'a small fish in a big pond'. It was now that my OCD was to be reborn. It seemed to be an undying parasite which could not be stopped by any amount of willpower.

The thoughts of death were still there though they shifted around to other subjects and eventually settled on the idea of me giving away my soul, a thought I found scary: to have myself owned by someone for an eternity. I would usually recite, 'I don't want to give my soul away'. To cover myself fully, it later evolved into 'I don't want to give my soul to anyone or anything no matter what happens' and finally the counting came in.

I would think to myself that I needed to tap something x

amount of times otherwise my soul would be taken away. It started off simply: 'I don't want to give my soul to anyone or anything as long as I tap this three times' – 'this' being any object that was near me. Three soon turned into five then ten then intricate sequences of numbers: 'three, seven, five, three'; 'five, seven, five, ten, five, seven, five'; 'five, seven, five, ten, nine, eight, seven, six, five, four, three, two, one, five, seven, five'. This was not as simple; I can tap at a speed of four taps a second but some of my sequences were adding up to almost 100 taps: that's 25 seconds of tapping. This was hard to keep up, especially if I lost count and had to start again.

The tapping is what I remember most about OCD. The patterns, sequences and numbers are all scrawled on my memory. The sequence which seemed to be most common, for reasons which I don't believe I'll ever know, was five, seven, five. This could be tapped in various ways. Often I would raise my hand from the surface and quickly tap it with each of my five fingers in quick succession making a short rattling noise: 'de de de de de'. That was the first five. Then I would raise my hand again (usually my right hand) and do the same: 'de de de de de'. Then I would lift my index finger and tap 'de (6) de (7)'. Finally I would tap the last five in the same way that I tapped the first.

This all might sound very complicated but I was a professional and could quickly do the five, seven, five sequence in about two to three seconds. All the other patterns could be tapped with extensions of this method. For example, ten taps would be two sets of five. Another pattern which arose as an extension to the standard five, seven, five was: five, seven, five, ten, five, seven, five.

If they went awry, these sequences would have to be restarted: 'one, two, three, four, five, one, two, three, four, five, six, seven, one, two, three, four, five, one, two, three, four, five, six, seven, eight, nine, ten, one, two, three, four, five, one, two, three, four, five, six, seven, one, two, three, five. Or was it four? Better start again. One, two, three' (and so on).

Then there was the whole dilemma of several different surfaces on one object. The tables at my school are much more complex structures than one might think. The main table was made of chipboard but this material was only visible from the underside of the table – the top had a glossy varnish on top of a thin layer of real wood. Around the edges were four strips of a third sort of wood, underneath which were four strips of metal welded to the four metal legs. So that's 14 different surfaces.

Say all these surfaces had to be tapped five, seven, five, ten, five, seven, five times, in order for me to leave the room – how many taps would that be? Well, it just so happens that I have a calculator to hand. Fourteen surfaces to be tapped. If I placed my fingers onto both surfaces I could tap the metal frame and the strips of wood around the edge at the same time so it was only ten surfaces:

$10 \times (5 + 7 + 5 + 10 + 5 + 7 + 5) =$ number of taps (T)

$10 \times 44 = T$

$T = 440$

FOUR HUNDRED AND FORTY TAPS! Just to leave my English class that I'd return to the next day! By the end of a five-lesson day I would have been well into quadruple figures, and that's only desks. What about chairs, door handles, doors, books, pens, food and more or less every other tangible object that I came in contact with? It's debatable at what point obsessive behaviour becomes OCD but I think most doctors would agree that thousands of taps a day means that you have a problem. I *should* have looked for help – '*should*' being the operative word.

This was something that I found impossible to explain to people and so I felt I had to keep it a secret. This went on for a couple of years until I was around 12 years old. So for two years I was all the time doing my very best to keep my secret from the world.

SUMMARY

» OCD can change from one form to another.
» Some people with OCD become obsessed with counting or doing certain things a certain number of times, or in a certain way.
» These numbers or number sequences may gradually get bigger and bigger, becoming more unmanageable.
» Irrational compulsions like this are referred to as 'rituals'.
» The numbers or number sequences are often triggered by thoughts that something bad will happen if the tapping is not carried out.
» These thoughts can be challenged by thinking to yourself, 'Nothing bad will happen whether I do this ritual or not!'.

Chapter 7

Keeping My Secret

When it is trodden on a worm will curl up. That is prudent. It thereby reduces the chance of being trodden on again.

- FRIEDRICH NIETZSCHE, TWILIGHT OF THE IDOLS

As my counting habit developed, I found ways of hiding it, while still being under its control. One example of this occurred when I was walking down the glass corridor in my school which connects the 'A' and 'B' block at what seemed to be rush hour. As I walked I ran my hand along the wooden rail that went along the side of the corridor, and as I approached the end of the rail the thought came into my head: 'I don't want to give my soul to anyone or anything as long as I tap this five, seven, five, ten, five, seven then five times'.

I began to tap this rail in the appropriate fashion and, as I was doing this, two of the older students came up behind me, pushed me, and started shouting abuse, asking me what I was doing. 'Nothing,' I said and walked on. Of course I had not completed the ritual so I went around the block and doubled back in order to complete it. This was but a temporary solution and it illustrates how OCD was becoming a bigger problem than just tapping – it had caused me to change my usual route and was becoming an obstacle in my life.

All the time, I was keeping it a secret. OCD is one of the best-kept secrets in the world and it is a problem which cannot be properly addressed if it remains this way. Go down to your local book shop and you will find several books on autism, depression or Asperger's syndrome but rarely any on OCD. Why is this? The main reason for it not coming to the surface is because people feel, first, that they are the only people who experience this and, second, that OCD is disturbingly obscure. Neither of these is true.

As I said earlier, OCD affects up to 2 in 100 people, so that rules the first reason out. Although to some people OCD may seem to be obscure, it is something that shares similar characteristics to everyday quite 'normal' worries. Most people worry about whether they have left electrical things on, even when they are sure that all is fine. However, I had not yet been enlightened with this knowledge.

For many with OCD, all rituals must be kept top secret like a government conspiracy. Our paranoia tells us that when people hear that you have a mental illness, the music from Hitchcock's *Psycho* will start up and the person that you are telling will run away to warn everyone else!

Misconceptions aside, what I did (and what I believe most other people in my situation would have done) was to do my best to hide my illness. People often run and tap their fingers along surfaces, so in cases where I was sitting down and still, I could do this, but when walking around I would have to find a reason to stop. A quick check of my mobile phone's message inbox, or a sudden thought that I had forgotten something followed by a realization that in fact I hadn't, were both good reasons to be momentarily still while I tapped whatever was necessary.

I can remember an incident on a holiday with a youth group where no excuse was available, and somebody asked me what I was doing. (I was tapping the field before we went in from a game of football.) I responded, 'What does it look like I'm doing? I'm poking the grass!' However, excuses did not help my condition and, in fact, camouflaging my compulsions only prolonged the time before I was able to receive treatment.

In conclusion I believe that my experience in trying to create secrecy is a cautionary tale, and that the less secret OCD is, the less a problem it will become. Those who have OCD must be able to recognize that it is OCD, and those who don't must be able to recognize it for the sake of others.

SUMMARY

» You will find lots of ways to try to hide OCD as it may seem embarrassing or weird.
» Hiding OCD is actually counterproductive.

Chapter 8

Learning to Walk the Walk

The simplest movements become fraught with risk and perplexity. Worst of all, you can no longer judge distances.

- ROGER POL-DROIT, 101 EXPERIMENTS IN THE PHILOSOPHY OF EVERYDAY LIFE (REFERRING TO THE SENSATION OF WALKING ACROSS A FAMILIAR ROOM IN THE DARK)

It had only been a couple of years since the tapping started but it was time again for a new branch of my OCD to develop. I must have been around 12 or 13, and it is said that when you become a teenager you feel the need to try new things, but this was ridiculous. Although tapping was a problem (and a big one), when I was walking in a straight line with nothing around me I was OK. That is until the thought came about that 'I don't want to give my soul to anyone or anything as long as I step on this surface only seven times'.

Some background information: the pathways in Hampshire where I live, along with a lot of England's pathways, are in a bad need of repair. There are re-cemented areas where drains have been mended and wires re-wired and most pathways have a long strip of cement down the middle where cable was installed and the company didn't clear up afterwards. This meant that there were lots of different surfaces for my OCD to cover: I would become trapped in a cycle between the different surfaces. Walking down paths, I would be stepping five then seven then five times, swapping floor surface, and then stepping five then seven then five times, swapping floor surface again, and so on. This created a swaying motion as I walked along which made it hard for me to walk in a group and meant that my OCD could be noticed much more easily.

I would often come to the end of a surface and be short of a few steps, so I would have to make up the steps with quick stamps, before going on to the next. If I had fallen short of steps, I would have to make either a quick leap to the safe floor surface or a shuffle of my feet so that they did not lift off the ground. There was also a secondary debate in my mind over whether a step that crossed a crack constituted one or two steps, given that my foot would touch on two paving slabs.

By this time I had developed many techniques to handle this strange way of walking. If I ran out of room for my steps I would stamp my feet quickly or pretend to have forgotten something, holding a tense and straight palm to my mouth. I would turn around and walk half my steps until pulling my wallet out of my pocket and pretending that I was embarrassed (easy, because I *was*), then turn back and walk the rest of my steps.

There were times when the thoughts would come through so strong that I would hardly be able to walk at all. I could not walk! OCD had taken from me the proper use of my legs and there was nothing I felt I could do about it. The thoughts just flowed into my head like Niagara Falls and I stood the same chance of stopping the thoughts as I would stopping the waterfall. When I could walk, on a good day, I was still not in a fit state to run or even to walk down to the shops on my own. The thoughts would cause me to make strange movements in order to fill up or not overflow the designated step count.

My parents were not used to seeing me moonwalk from concrete to grass and therefore started to ask questions: 'Why were you swaying?' 'Why don't you walk properly?' I managed to dodge my way around the questions for a long time until it was time for us to go on a 'holiday of a lifetime' to Corfu, an exotic Greek island which presented me with yet more challenges for my OCD.

SUMMARY

» Sometimes OCD may make you walk a certain way or count the steps that you walk.

Chapter 9

OCD Abroad

I don't want to give my soul to anyone or anything if I tap this five, seven, five, ten, five, seven then five times.

– JOE WELLS' MIND, CORFU

I arrived at the airport at three o'clock in the morning and was very tired. I had spent the 'night' at a nearby hotel and then been transported by the hotel's coach service to the airport. The scene was busy, with confused people trying to understand vague instructions, police officers looking through people's bags and men buying several CDs in order to avoid tax.

The busy scene had a strong effect on my OCD. I would not be returning to this departure area and so was compelled to tap things. Around this time my OCD was focused on floors, so I was always checking my shoelaces in order to tap the floor the appropriate amount of times. This held us up on the way, and my parents rushed me towards the plane.

The plane journey was not too bad, being in the same place for a long time (that is to say my OCD was not too bad – the plane made my ears pop and the food tasted like sawdust). I arrived at Corfu airport and left there on a coach, and as I was getting more and more nervous, my OCD got worse and worse.

We settled into our apartment, checked out the pool, and that evening decided to go to the nearby restaurant 'The Three Little Pigs'. After I had finished my plate of spaghetti, the plate was there sitting in front of me, within a foot of my chest. I folded my arms tightly in front of me and tried not to tap the plate, in the knowledge that once in a cycle of taps, I would not be able to get out. But still the thoughts came into my head. 'No, no, I don't want to tap the plate,' I tried to say, but the overwhelming thoughts of 'I want to give my soul away unless I tap this plate five then seven then five times' were too powerful.

As I tapped the plate, my mind was distracted with the counting of the tapping and so I lowered my defences: the thoughts could add more numbers 'then ten then five then seven then five again' and would never stop as long as I was tapping – I was trapped in a never-ending cycle.

I eventually managed to stop the strings of numbers by thinking 'and then never again after that' after a number. You can imagine how exhausting this all was for me.

As I was tapping this plate, my parents (who had recognized that I was doing these things but had not worked up the courage to ask me why I was doing them) took it upon themselves to remove the plate from me. In this instance, I was just finishing the appropriate sequence as the plate was being taken away, but on other occasions I would lean across the table to tap the plate with my parents trying to stop me. This was quite noticeable to other people in the restaurant as a tussle between me and my parents would result, as they tried to pull the plate away and I was pulling it back. A lot of unnecessary hostility was generated from these incidents. My parents were trying to help me so I had no reason to be angry at them, and I did not want to be doing these things so my parents had no reason to be angry at me. But I would find myself being angry with my parents, saying, 'Why can't you just let me tap it? It's not doing you any harm,' to which they would reply, 'But you don't *need* to do it'. My compulsions were very strong, which I can now see by the unreasonable way in which I responded to my parents genuinely trying to help me.

As I walked home, because I was so tired and my mind could not contradict the OCD successfully, I began to be almost unable to walk at all. When I could I was unstable with my steps and began to meander drunkenly (not that I looked out of place among the other British tourists). If I linked arms with one of my parents, I could walk in a straight line, yet still I would be either stamping my feet or making exaggerated strides and this meant that my parents did not want to walk with me. It was becoming much harder for me to keep control of my OCD. I eventually got to the apartment and went to sleep in the knowledge that the next 13 days would be exactly the same.

One method which I had developed to try to 'block out' the thoughts, which had been successful in the past, was reciting a contradicting thought while my OCD was trying to make me think the thought linked with the compulsion. If I thought, 'I don't want to give my soul to anyone as long as I tap this table five, then seven, then five times', I would deliberately and confidently say in my head, 'I don't want to give my soul to anyone or anything, whatever happens or wherever I am!' This covered everything and it was just a thought I had to do in my head; I didn't have to lift a finger. I tried to use this in Corfu but often the compulsion-related thoughts were just too strong and I couldn't block them out.

Later that week we visited another restaurant. It was positioned on the edge of a cliff so that we could absorb the beauty of the sunset whilst inhaling the secondary smoke of fellow diners. I had finished my meal and we were about to leave. All the plates were piled on the other side of the table but I was still tapping the underside of the table. In my thoughts I had lined up a series of taps for the table underside, and then had to tap the straw, which had been levitated from the base of my glass by the bubbles from the lemonade. It poked towards me and into my obsessive thoughts. I had not yet finished the long series of taps when my parents decided it was time to go back to our apartment. They felt that it would help me to pull me away from the table. However, I managed to grab the straw and tap it on my way to the car, without my parents knowing.

On reflection, although drastic, and somewhat embarrassing, the way that my parents tried to prevent me from being able to fulfil my rituals was a helpful method, which helped me to challenge OCD. To be prevented from carrying out a ritual, and then being able to find out that the intense anxiety does eventually fade away, was something that helped me manage my OCD and the fears that were associated with it, but only as part of a more wide-ranging strategy.

Later that week I went down to the arcade with my parents who were becoming increasingly concerned about me and my bizarre rituals. My dad inserted a coin into the slot of a basketball game. The wooden gate electronically went up and two cheap basketballs rolled down towards us. For a few minutes my family threw the basketballs towards the net, usually missing. As you would expect, I was tapping the basketballs in the appropriate sequences every time they came to me. Towards the end of the given time, my parents had realized what I was doing and were nagging me to stop. On what I didn't realize was my last shot, I was halfway through tapping the ball when it was snatched off me by my dad. It missed the net and was stopped by the gate which descended whilst the ball was in mid-air.

During this incident the thoughts had been so strong; I had not been able to block them in my head and I felt a need to fulfil the compulsion. Therefore, later that week, I went back to the game and paid to tap the ball again.

When my OCD was at a less severe level, I found out that incidents like these are in fact extremely good to help one convince oneself of how ridiculous the obsessions are. I found that subjecting myself to this nagging feeling that would arise when a compulsion was unfulfilled by me was very helpful, especially towards the end of my recovery. However, at this point I was so influenced by the urgency of my compulsions, I had to satisfy them.

The rest of the holiday continued in the same tradition; in the evenings I would be tired and would find it harder to stop the thoughts from entering my mind. Ironically it is at this time that I would generally be leaving my plates, cutlery, tables, tablecloths, glasses, etc., all of which had to be tapped in the appropriate sequence. Every night I'd stagger home, being pulled along by my parents, as I was trying to finish off my steps on the edge of a pavement. If I held my parent's hand this was a useful way of managing the OCD as I felt that I was not in control of the pace at which I was walking, and the stepping thoughts were easier to block out. This I realize now is only a temporary solution as I was relinquishing the responsibility to my parents and not really tackling the OCD myself. And also, although I was 12 at the time, holding your parent's hand was not a cool thing to do, even if I was in a foreign country.

In contrast to these negative experiences, on a day trip to a monastery in the south of Corfu, I did find one of the most helpful pieces of equipment to someone with OCD. I am quite cynical of such alternative practices as acupuncture, herbal medicine and magnetic therapy. However, outside this monastery I came across this instrument called a set of 'worry beads'. They look similar to a rosary but have one long line of about 30 beads. The idea is that if you are worried about something, you count the beads and your mind concentrates on counting them; then when you have finished you can reassess your worry more logically. These beads were really helpful and I would recommend that people with OCD keep something on them to count, or alternatively when OCD is bothering you, find something pointless to count like floor tiles or the eyelets on your shoes. This helps you to challenge OCD in the ways that will follow later in the book. The beads did not help me at the time, but later on they proved very useful.

It was near the end of the holiday that I was first informed that OCD is an illness, and that other people had it. My mum had obviously not done her homework very well because she identified it as OCB, 'Obsessive Compulsive Behaviour', a term I have never heard since. She didn't tell me much else, but I was relieved to know that it was a recognized difficulty and that other people had it. My younger sister, Emma, had recently been upset by my behaviour, especially after the restaurant debacle earlier in the week. My mum persuaded me to go and talk to my sister. I explained to my sister that it was because I sometimes got very nervous, and that that was how I coped with it. This helped to normalize my sometimes frighteningly weird behaviour. She accepted what I said and, as she revealed later, was comforted by the knowledge that I wasn't going mad. I definitely feel it was helpful to share this information with my sister and helped in the future for her to understand more easily what I was going through, and why, and to be able to help me in my fight against the OCD.

SUMMARY

» The people who care about you will struggle themselves, having to watch you struggle.

» Give your parents feedback on what helps you and what doesn't. They're only human and probably don't know what it's like, so guide them.

» Be aware of holidays. OCD can thrive in unfamiliar situations. However, this doesn't mean that you should avoid them; just be prepared.

Chapter 10

Getting Help

My therapist asked me to describe my recurring anxiety dream about running a marathon, I said, 'I don't know where to start.'

– MARK SIMMONS

After the Corfu trauma, my parents told me that the previous autumn they had spoken to my usual GP, who had recognized my symptoms as OCD and had written to the Child and Family Therapy Team near me in order to 'refer' me to them. My parents had apparently met with a doctor there, and talked about my difficulties, but because of my reluctance to admit that anything was wrong had been unable to take things any further. I did not see this referral until I started writing this book, and several items are referred to in what seems to me a new light.

Patient: Mr. Wells DOB: 17 Feb 1989 29 November 2000

Dear Team

I would be very grateful for your assessment of this young man who I have serious concerns about. He seems to suffer from an extreme anxiety over many issues which is bordering on paranoia on some occasions. In the past he has had episodes of repetitive behaviour and obsessive behaviour but these were very short lived and associated with a stressful event in his life. The present crisis has been brought on by going up to [senior school] last September but does not show any signs of settling; in fact things are getting worse. He has ritualistic behaviour for a number of things, particularly first thing in the morning when he is leaving home. He has been given a small bracelet by his church group and since receiving it has felt unable to remove it and at the present he is hiding it and seems quite terrified about removing it.

Previous problems have included repetitive hand washing, concern about poisoning in foods, being concerned about being near batteries because of poisoning, etc. He recently had an episode of agitation but we believe this may have been due to having steroids for asthma. All the rest of his symptoms predate this. Looking back in his notes the first real problems were reported in January 1999 but certainly the number of episodes and the length of problems is increasing. On all previous occasions the family have been very resistant to getting a team involved. The mother works as a behavioural therapist with disturbed children and knows a lot of treatments but really feels that this is beyond her resources and help. I am concerned that this lad might have early OCD and I would be very grateful for your assessment.

The wrist band that the letter refers to was given to me by the church, after a talk on how we should have a reminder of our faith on our bodies (like a cross or a fish). I put on this wristband, and had a seemingly logical assumption that I was in some way better off keeping this band on (continuously for a whole year).

This caused problems in PE lessons, with teachers always telling me that I should take it off, in case of the somewhat unlikely chance that someone's finger could get stuck in it when running, and the band would rip it off. This bemused me, as in comparison to the other injuries I sustained in rugby lessons, a lost finger would have been the least of my worries.

This habit, I have found out, is a common trait among people with OCD. Some people become obsessed with lucky charms, or objects to ensure safety and security, yet this compulsion I felt was very easy to throw off once I had taken the band off. Each second without the band that I did not spend enduring horrible tortures was more evidence that I was safe without the band. I took the band off, and none of the horrific things which I believed possible have happened to this day. For people who have these compulsions, I feel that the way to counsel yourself out of the feeling of the object's necessity is very much the obvious: to leave the objects at home, or at least not have them on you, for as long a period of time as feels comfortable. My dad encouraged me to take off the wrist band, at first for just half an hour at a time, then hours, then I took it off forever, but still kept it in a safe place.

So my doctor sent the letter to the Child and Family Therapy Team nearby, and my first appointment came quite quickly. What should I expect? All I knew about 'therapy' was what I'd seen on TV. I was under the impression that my therapist would be an eccentric middle-aged man, with long hair, who wore slippers to work, and that he would always be checking the time. (This is an American thing because the American equivalent of the NHS is quite modest and most therapy and counselling is done privately.) I also thought that I would be asked to sit on one of those long chairs shaped like a lower-case 'L' with the leather exterior pulled tightly into little leather buttons. But none of this was true! It was not what I expected when Alison Wallis, Clinical Psychologist, led me into a simple room furnished with those padded chairs, with the chunky frames, that you sometimes get in the front bit of Chinese restaurants.

I didn't know what was going to happen at the appointment, as I did not yet know, and to an extent still don't know, how similar one OCD case is to another. The treatment I was to be given was called CBT or Cognitive Behavioural Therapy. Breaking down that abbreviation which may seem meaningless: 'Cognitive' is when things are based in empirical facts and solid evidence. 'Behavioural' means the things that we do, in my case repetitive tapping. And 'Therapy' is a word for treatment which does not involve physical intervention from a doctor, so in other words there wasn't to be any medicine or scalpels involved. So the doctor was going to make my actions be rational and based on evidence. In theory, the problem was that I was so embedded in

OCD (which we know is completely irrational) I could barely tell the difference between what was rational and what wasn't. I did genuinely believe that my soul could be taken away. Who by? It was unclear. But the belief was so strong, it seemed almost a fact. It was as though at the same time as OCD was consuming my life, it was also consuming my understanding of logic, and science.

I was going to go through with it. Alison seemed sincere that she didn't think that I was a lost cause, so I thought that we might as well try. My only concern was if they'd got it wrong and I didn't have OCD, but manic depression, schizophrenia, or whatever Norman Bates had. I had never heard of people having these thoughts, so did not know if my case was unique. My concerns were reassured by Alison understanding what I was saying and even further by a CD-ROM which I was given called *Why Me?* which I thoroughly recommend to anyone with OCD. First it has a Pulp song on its soundtrack and second when I put on the disc I realized for the first time that lots of other people struggled in the same way that I did. There was a whole computer screen of young people with OCD and they must have just been the adolescents who wanted to be in it from one hospital. I thought this was amazing: I was not the only one who had this and these people who I'd never met were going through the same thing as I was. That CD is probably hard to find now, but there are loads of videos where people talk about their OCD on the OCD-UK website (OCDUK.org).

So there I was in this room, with the doctor who my parents had talked to, and Alison Wallis who I would do most of the CBT with. For the first couple of weeks she mainly listened to my account of pretty much everything up until this sentence. The OCD was so deep and complex that it was very hard to explain. But after a few weeks I got the impression that Alison pretty much understood where I was coming from. So the CBT could begin. Alison was often asking me to give evidence for and against the ideas behind the compulsions, and for the specific fear of losing my soul. The two sides were as follows:

If I do not tap [the item] x amount of times my soul will be removed because:

- I have agreed that it should happen in my head so it is arranged for my soul to be taken.
- I have always tapped and therefore I'm being kept safe.
- Other people don't lose theirs because they don't have the thoughts.
- Even if I don't lose my soul straightaway somebody could claim it later.
- If I think something then it is the same as doing it (in accordance with Christianity).
- It's not worth the risk for just this one time.

If I do not tap [the item] nothing will happen because:

- I don't want it to be taken away and it is mine to give therefore no one can take it.
- I have been unable to tap things in the past and my soul is still here.
- It is not me that has said that I have to do it, it is my OCD.
- If I don't want my soul to be taken then it can't be.
- My soul can't be owned by anyone as it is my own consciousness. If it is owned it ceases to exist.
- The OCD has control of me which is what my fear is, so if I do not tap then my soul is more free.

I had to learn to believe the second list so that when the thoughts came I could simply say to myself 'no one can "own" my soul so these thoughts are ridiculous' but this was very hard, especially at school and when I was stressed. These theories of challenging OCD had to be put into practice and had to be perfected for use in my daily life. I had to persuade myself that the positive beliefs were true; however, I found myself very hard to convince.

My OCD also now decided to place another cruel hand on me and control another part of my body. My mind was for obsessive thoughts, my feet were for obsessive walks, my hands were for obsessive taps, and now my eyes were for obsessive blinks. The thought wasn't that I had to blink a certain amount of times but it might as well have been. It was that I had to look at something a certain amount of times. For example, let's pick something obscure: 'I must look at that kiwi fruit in the fruit bowl five times. Well, I'm already looking at it, so if I blink with both eyes once, then again, then again, then again, I've blinked four times but have looked at the kiwi five times. So as to round up the ritual so that I've only looked at it five times I must close my eyes then turn my head away whilst my eyes are still closed then open them again with the kiwi out of sight. That's all well and good until the rituals get longer, with bigger numbers, complex sequences and numerous objects. I don't need to go into detail as you should know by now that OCD is never quite as simple as it might first appear.

This was one of the most obvious things which OCD made me do. Often people who have other illnesses like Tourette's syndrome develop facial tics which look similar to what I was doing. So I was appearing as if I had a completely different illness, which isn't really a good thing when I want people to be able to support me and want to fit in with people.

SUMMARY

» Get your GP to refer you on to a therapist or someone else who can help you.

» Modern therapists are not like they are on TV; it's much more relaxed and nothing to worry about.

» Don't be embarrassed to tell these specialists about the things that OCD makes you think or do; they will have heard similar things before.

» Having help with combating OCD does help a lot! It can feel virtually impossible to overcome OCD on your own.

» A therapist is not the same as other doctors; you have to help yourself too. There is no miracle pill that cures you on its own.

Chapter 11

Convincing Myself of OCD's Irrationality

gadji beri bimba glandridi laula lonni cadori

- HUGO BALL, GADJI BERI BIMBA

Have you seen the film *The Wicker Man*, where towards the end, Constable Howie shouts at the village people (trying to save himself from being sacrificed), 'Can't you see, there is no "sun god", there is no "goddess of the fields"?' Howie sees that the beliefs of the villagers are completely ridiculous; he knows that human sacrifice won't help their harvest. But Lord Summerisle and the villagers are so caught up in their beliefs that they cannot accept what Howie is saying.

I watched that film about a year ago when I was beginning to be able to control my OCD and can remember a strange feeling of déjà vu. I realized that this scene had taken place in my head – 'rationality' being Howie and 'OCD' as Lord Summerisle. I had been saying to myself, 'Can't you see, you can't have your soul taken just because you didn't tap something?' It was like talking to a particularly unresponsive brick wall. I knew, partly because of Alison convincing me, yet mainly because of my own common sense, that I did not have to carry out the rituals and that nothing would happen to me if I didn't. However, I could not stop carrying them out! One thing which I can't stress enough is that OCD is completely nonsensical and will not listen to reason. This is one of the most frightening things about having it. I knew that to anyone I told, there are Salvador Dali paintings that make more sense.

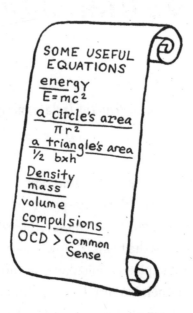

SOME USEFUL EQUATIONS

$$\frac{energy}{E=mc^2}$$

$$\frac{a\ circle's\ area}{\pi r^2}$$

$$\frac{a\ triangle's\ area}{\frac{1}{2}\ bxh}$$

$$\frac{Density}{mass}$$

volume

$$\frac{compulsions}{OCD > Common\ Sense}$$

Just as I found it hard to convince my OCD of its own irrationality, so did other people; my mum, dad and Alison were the only people who really knew at this point. My sister saw my compulsions but did not know about the thoughts behind them. None of these people could convince me, or at least could not convince my OCD, that it was irrational. People I have met who have known other people with OCD have often expressed a feeling of frustration with them which I can sympathize with, as I felt the same frustration myself with OCD. What people do not realize is that the person with OCD is frustrated too, even more so than someone that just has to be around them.

Alison contacted a chaplain in 2002 when I must have been 13 and I was given a letter in which the chaplain answers some questions that Alison put to him on my behalf.

Alison contacted the chaplain in mid-April and asked the following:

1. Can you make losing your soul dependent on something?
2. Is it a belief held in the church that someone else can own your soul and, if this were to be the case, do you know how you may lose it?

The chaplain answered:

1. Losing your soul doesn't depend on anything, and nobody in the church believes that tapping could keep your soul safe.
2. Although some cultures believe other people can own your soul, the church does not share this belief. The church believes that no person could own another's soul and that the soul cannot be removed.

So the church provides evidence that my thoughts are irrational; the doctors say that my thoughts are irrational; my own logical thinking says that my thoughts are irrational; and I'm sure that if I spoke to a lawyer they would say that an obsessive thought is not a legally binding contract. So all the experts said that these thoughts were ludicrous, nonsensical and absurd. 'Look,' I said to my OCD, 'you are wrong, biblically, scientifically, philosophically and legally, you are wrong! These rituals mean nothing. I could never perform another ritual in my life and still my soul would be my own.' But all this evidence, weighted with tons of authority, was not enough to persuade my OCD. OCD bears a sad delusion of its own infallibility: it was stubborn, and it would not budge.

Alison, Mum and Dad's reasoning was logical and rational, yet futile against OCD. At this point this kind of help was useless because OCD was like a great wall that could not be broken down; it was omnipotent and infallible. So a slightly different approach was needed.

One idea was just to think over the thoughts or sing a song in my head. This does work and can be helpful, but it stops you from doing other very simple things like having a conversation and it does not stop the thoughts from creeping up on you unexpectedly. As a technique it is temporary and in no way the solution itself; it did not challenge the OCD but just made it harder for it to infiltrate my brain. I later decided that this should only be used at the times when OCD was too strong for me to use other methods.

The next method was to be challenging and new to me. It would be stronger and (I hoped) it would work.

SUMMARY

» OCD is a very silly illness: the things that it makes you do make no sense but to someone who has OCD they seem to make a lot of sense.

» It is hard to convince someone with OCD that it is silly, but an expert can teach a person how to be more rational.

Chapter 12

Challenging

Arguments are a lot like buses, you mainly get into them at bus stops

– MATT WINNING

'Challenging' is described in my dictionary as provoking a 'contest duel' which is a nice way of saying 'a row'. Not necessarily the type of row which might have your neighbours complaining, but a row all the same. Because OCD had its own irrational set of rules that differed a great deal from the rules I was using with the CBT approach to challenge it, OCD was hard to reason with. The basic idea was as follows. When the thoughts come into your mind, instead of fulfilling the rituals say to yourself, 'NO, I don't need to do that because nothing bad will really happen to me if I don't', then the thoughts will lose their validity and the anxiety will leave.

When I first tried this, my OCD would not listen! I felt like I was talking to a bigot. I gave it reason, I gave it valid answers to its argument, but still the OCD remained. Its argument was stupid and made no sense, but OCD speaks louder than sense. So this primitive challenging did not work, especially as a means to climb out from the deep pit in which I found myself.

Perhaps this kind of challenge could work in mild OCD cases, but I was going to be using industrial-strength CBT.

One method which is very helpful yet somewhat uncomfortable is *writing down* why OCD is incorrect. I did this with Alison and I'm doing it now. I had my argument in writing, which OCD didn't have. I don't know why this gave me more strength but it did, and I would recommend it to others.

I had two options. OCD was a two-part process: (1) the thoughts and (2) the actions.

Thoughts ➡ Actions

I could try to stop the actions so that, although I'd still be having the obsessive thoughts, that would be it, the end.

Thoughts ➡ ???

This would mean that a block would have to be placed in between the thoughts and the actions. But what could this block be? It would have to go against the thoughts and make them less powerful, so it would not be the thoughts *leading to* something other than compulsions but the thoughts being *blocked by* something other than compulsions.

Thoughts ➡ ??? (nothing leads to actions so they do not happen)

This block had to be something in my head or another thought. There had to be something that I could think that would stop the OCD thoughts. I'm not going to make things out to be easier than they are or suggest that I can give all the answers, as I never found a foolproof method. Writing helped, 'brainstorming' reasons why I shouldn't have to do the actions helped, and deliberate reasoned contradiction of the thoughts helped.

Another helpful yet slightly less conventional technique which I was taught was relaxation. When relaxation is mentioned people think of Buddhist monks, incense sticks and panpipe music, so when Alison told me that we were going to do relaxation I was slightly perturbed, but she joked that she didn't have any CDs of whale music so I felt slightly more at ease.

A great by-product of OCD is anxiety and stress, so I guess that relaxation is a good way to go. I went to the session knowing that I would be doing it, but I didn't exactly know what 'it' was.

Leaning back on my chair, first I had to tense my feet really tightly then relax them. Then I had to tense my legs and make them as straight as possible with my lifeless feet drooping down at the bottom. Then I relaxed my legs and they sunk into the chair. I had to tense my bum and torso then relax them. Then I did the same for my arms. I had to sit in the chair for a few minutes and then get up and leave the room without tapping. My stress levels would be measured from one to ten, one being completely free from the thoughts all the way up to ten which was unbearable, and I could use these to measure which methods were most effective against OCD. The first experiment in which the stress level test was used went as follows. Sit down for 30 seconds, get up, touch the door and come back. First during silence, then whilst talking to someone (something which also helps combat OCD as it helps you to focus on the conversation). Then, after the relaxation exercises. Here are the results that I had:

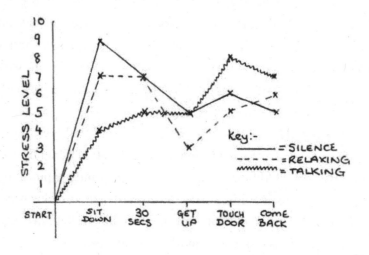

10 – ABSOLUTE HELL!

9 – Strong anxiety

8 – Anxious

7 – Quite anxious

6 – A bit uncomfortable

5 – OK

4 – Quite relaxed

3 – Relaxed

2 – Very relaxed

1 – Cool as a cucumber.

The results are fairly mixed and like I said earlier there is no miracle cure for OCD. One reason why medication for OCD has been given a bad name is because people naively believe it to be a cure, but it isn't. It was clear from these results and my own experience that I was going to have to create a hybrid of methods in order to control the problem. The 'one to ten' method can be used easily and is very useful if you have someone who is trying to help you through OCD; you can whisper the number to them and they know how anxious you are feeling. Feel free to copy and use my thermometer.

I found this scale very useful when trying to show people how I was feeling and keep track of my emotions. During the bulk of my OCD my anxiety would usually measure at about seven or eight when everything was going OK, but sometimes, particularly during the evening or when I was leaving somewhere, it would rise to nine or ten. At certain points, like leaving the restaurants in Corfu, I felt like I was in treble figures! So I was well organized; I knew the facts, I knew the methods and now I had some kind of measuring device. What else would I need in my OCD-prevention kit-bag?

It was around this time when the idea of taking medication began to be talked about. 'Medication' is the sugar-coated word for 'drugs'. At first I was unsure. I had been told all my life that drugs are bad for you, and was scared by what these drugs would be doing exactly. The word 'drug' covers quite a wide group ranging from a single ibuprofen to an overdose of heroin. At what point between those two were my 'drugs' going to be? In other words how drastic would the effects of these drugs be? Should I keep practising my CBT?

I started to get into discussions with the Child and Family Therapy team and we seemed to be making a lot of progress then WHAM! Something else hit me.

SUMMARY

- » Cognitive Behavioural Therapy (CBT) is used to treat OCD. CBT helps you change your behaviour so that it is based on solid facts and sound logic.
- » You can use this sound logic and solid facts to challenge the OCD thoughts.
- » Therapists can train you in CBT, but it's up to you to use it.
- » You can measure your anxiety from one to ten using a gauge; this helps to show other people how you are feeling.

Chapter 13

Depression and OCD

What's the good of being a giant if you're smaller than everybody and can't frighten anybody?

– ROBERT KRAUS, THE LITTLE GIANT

If there is a god, then apparently I had done something to offend him. I was scurrying around frantically trying to get my life back together against the will of OCD when I 'entered' adolescence. People's image of teenagers is very similar to comedian Harry Enfield's character 'Kevin the teenager': listening to punk rock, going to parties and shouting 'It's so unfair!' at your parents. OCD created a distorted teenager with elements of the stereotype, elements of my own personality and elements of OCD. It was as though someone had taken 'Kevin', Joe Wells and OCD, and moulded them into a new person.

Adolescence is a lot harder than it is made out to be, especially when you've got OCD. Homework, friends, family, household chores, exams, girls, clothes, self-identity: it was all too much! Just as I was climbing out of a pit of OCD, adolescence dragged me back in. I was already in a dodgy way because of OCD and now teenage hormones were messing things up. This adolescence/OCD concoction was not something to be served up at dinner parties. A mixture of two chemical imbalances destroyed my senses, as though I was on some dangerous drug.

There's a lot of helpful advice out there on this subject and if you really want to go into detail try reading *From Thoughts to Obsessions* by Per Hove Thomsen or browsing around www. OCDaction.org.uk. I have had it explained to me that some scientists believe that OCD is caused by an imbalance of a chemical substance called serotonin in your brain, which would imply that OCD has a biological cause. Adolescence is also caused by the excretion of hormone chemicals into one's bloodstream. If I've got these two chemical imbalances causing me to think unreasonably, how am I supposed to act reasonably?

As an example of my strange behaviour, my parents might ask me to hang up my coat if I'd forgotten to; this would, in my mind (which was only one third Joe Wells), be inflated into a much bigger issue as though I was being penalized by my parents and as though they were looking for a reason to be condescending towards me. It seemed as though the smallest molehill would end up as Mount Everest in my mind. I was worried about my social status, yet in a much more exaggerated and paranoid way than most teenagers. I really didn't want to phone my friends and ask if they wanted to go out for fear of rejection. The events of most evenings spent at home would escalate into a full-scale argument with my family and I was too scared to call my friends to spend my evenings in any other way.

I felt as though every day was the same: you get up, do things which are predictable, inevitable and pointless, then go back to sleep, only to do exactly the same things the next day. What was the point of anything? I was always unhappy and sometimes I would find myself sad for no particular reason. At this time my parents had become worried about me again and as Alison had gone on maternity leave I was now seeing someone else who was a counselling psychologist. It wasn't long before this came up in the sessions at Child and Family Therapy. In one of my calm moments my mum got me to write down the things I was upset about, and they were as follows:

1. I feel angry often and shout. I feel tense, worried and sad.
2. My OCD is better than in the first place but worse than it was a few months ago.
3. I can't concentrate at school and I feel tired.
4. I can't sleep and I wake up during the night.

The OCD Recycling Scheme

STRESS

OCD

THOUGHTS → ACTIONS

Turn your unwanted stress
into (unwanted) compulsions

The word 'depression' had been circling around me like a vulture and was finally labelled by my mum who had been affected by it when she was younger and also felt that she could relate my outlook on life to hers as a teenager.

When you are diagnosed with 'depression' it is as though you have been branded with a horrifically unfair stereotype. During the time that I was 'depressed' I never self-harmed, took illegal drugs or attempted suicide. If you'd met me at a party you would not have thought of me as being depressed as I was not shy or unconfident in talking to people. I would never appear sad when I was with my friends or at school; it was only when I was at home. When it didn't show was when my depression felt at its worst.

All the bad things that happened to me seemed to be much bolder in my head than the good things. My mum suggested that I should keep a diary of all the good things that happened to me so that my attention would be drawn closer to them. I said that I did not feel that there were any 'good things' to write down so she said to me, 'Well, let's just write down the things that aren't actually bad', so that was what I did. I filled the diary with small trivial things which at least weren't bad. One day I went out with friends; one day I went to the cinema with my family; one day I went to a party. All of a sudden my life didn't seem quite as miserable as it previously had done. This was a brilliant idea and it was certainly one of a few things that helped me get through depression. Another thing which I believe helped me has always been a somewhat controversial subject: taking medication for depression and OCD.

SUMMARY

> » OCD can really get you down, so collaborates well with depression as when you feel down OCD gets worse and vice versa.
> » Depression is more than just having a bad day; it can really affect your life.
> » Lots of teenagers may feel down because of hormones and this can be part of adolescence.
> » If depression is, in your opinion, becoming a problem and inflaming OCD you should tell someone, preferably a therapist if you are seeing one.

Chapter 14

Citalopram

I want to use comedy to lift the lid on anti-depressants but it's hard because first you've got to push it down and click it round.

– LAURA LEXX

It became clear that on its own CBT was not going to be enough to stop the overpowering OCD thoughts and depression. The counselling psychologist and my parents had asked me in the past whether I would consider medication but I had always refused as I wanted to use my own willpower and CBT.

However, I now feel that I was not properly informed about what medication I would be taking and what effect it would have on me. I knew absolutely nothing. Would it be tablets or liquid medicine? Would I still have to use CBT? Would it have any side effects? I could not possibly have been expected to make an 'informed' decision as I had not been informed. My fears were that either I would feel artificially 'happy' and would walk around wearing a big false smile or that my feelings would be deadened and I wouldn't feel like 'myself' any more. So I refused to consider medication and my parents were told by the psychologist I was seeing at that time that it was my decision not to take medication, and my parents felt unable to take it any further.

Eventually I ended up seeing a psychiatrist at Child and Family Therapy, and this time when my parents asked about medication, I was told about citalopram. The psychiatrist told me that I could try the tablets for a couple of months (it takes about six weeks before they work properly anyway) and if I wasn't happy with taking them and they didn't help then I could be eased back off the tablets at any time. (You have to ease yourself on and off the tablets, starting with a small amount and then working up, then if you want to come off you have to work your way down.) This seemed like a reasonable plan and they also told me more about side effects and intentional effects.

It all now appeared to be not that bad. I was told that I would have to use CBT as well and that it wasn't going to take over my mind or make me have any extra unwanted thoughts. So I thought I'd give it a go. I was prescribed citalopram and eventually the tablets arrived at my pharmacy and I had them there in my hand, with a glass of water in the other. After some hesitation I took them and went out and did whatever I was doing that day. At this point I was only on 10 milligrams. Twenty milligrams is the suggested dose for depression for adults, but I was later to go up to 40 for the OCD.

When you first start taking medication like this, it is very hard to know what is real and what is a placebo. I felt happier that day and my OCD wasn't that bad, but even before that I sometimes had good days – how did I know what was what? At first, I couldn't tell if the medicine was working. But over a longer course of time it became much clearer. I was using the tactics that I had been taught as strongly as I could and, although I had bad days, it seemed to me after a few weeks on 10, then 20 milligrams, that things generally were beginning to get better. It seemed to be a lot easier to ignore the depressing thoughts and everything seemed to be going well.

The truth was that in fact things were exactly the same and it was just my outlook that was different. When I go down town with my friends and we're in the amusements arcade it doesn't seem incredibly exciting to me. However, I see young children there with their parents and to them it seems like the most exciting place in the world. In a similar way, I was now seeing things with a much more positive outlook. It didn't mean that I was not susceptible to pain (in the same way as if a child gets split up from their parents in the arcade or trips over): things still upset me. I would still get annoyed if something bad happened in the same way that any person would. But I did not seem to be in the inescapable pit of depression that I was in before.

Things improved because I had gained this confidence through a combination of challenging depression and the citalopram and was able to phone up my friends. I hadn't been able to do this before. It in turn meant that my friends phoned me much more. I talked to people more in class, which began to get me in trouble on occasions. I made lots of new friends and had an active social life; in fact I still do. Friends that I made after coming out of depression have said to me that they couldn't understand me beforehand and didn't know why I didn't talk to them.

So things were great; I'd overcome my depression and it had only taken me a few months. But I was only scraping at the surface of the problem and the next issue was going to be much bigger. OCD was still there, in me. Its presence remained strong and I decided that I was going to have to get rid of it, especially now that I had friends to notice it.

In order to handle OCD it was recommended that I should go up to 40 milligrams of citalopram, which is quite high, but I would need all the help I could get. It was as though I was preparing myself for a battle against OCD, which had always bullied me around and told me what to do. Now I was going to try to make it go away.

So I went up to 30, then 40, milligrams and was challenging the OCD, striking it back as it lunged at me. I'd fall down and OCD would dishonourably attack me while I was in that state, yet with CBT and the medicine I could get up again. I strongly agree with Nietzsche's idea that what does not kill us makes us stronger. I was desperate to get rid of OCD and the more experience I had, the better I was at beating it. I was getting stronger and stronger. My parents and my psychiatrist saw this and we decided, being the keen scientists that we are, that we ought to conduct some experiments to log my progress and to deliberately put me in situations where my OCD would be severe.

You will see that this is a useful way of assessing the strength of OCD and reducing its influence.

Experiment 1: Bottle recycling

Hypothesis: If a human with OCD takes bottles to the recycling bin his OCD will be stronger than usual and will compel him to hold on to the bottles. Even stronger CBT will block out the OCD and enable him to throw away the bottles.

Equipment: Green recycling bin, plastic bottles, OCD, human specimen.

Method: Joe must take the bottles to the recycling bin at the end of his drive. He knows that when the bottles are taken away he will never see them again and never be able to ritually tap them again. Joe's OCD will cause him to be compelled to tap the bottles in the appropriate order. However, he has been given citalopram and has been taught how to use CBT. Therefore this experiment aims to prove or disprove the following equation:

CBT + Citalopram > OCD

We know that OCD is of variable strength, and in this situation we feel that it will be of high strength due to Joe's knowledge of where the bottles are going. However, we also know that at this time Joe has developed a skilful use of CBT which we think that, in conjunction with the citalopram, should override OCD.

Results: The experiment showed that the specimen's use of CBT was very well conducted and that although OCD caused a rise in anxiety levels OCD did not occur because Joe's willpower prevented the OCD. Further similar experiments found that anxiety levels (measured on a scale of one to ten) reduced the more times the experiment was conducted.

From this we conclude that exposure to higher doses of OCD than one is used to builds up an immunity to the anxiety caused by OCD and therefore makes OCD easier to overcome.

Experiment 2: Selling the family car

Hypothesis: OCD is made stronger by putting human in a situation where he is to part with a car that he has been a passenger in for several years. Even stronger CBT will have to be used by human.

Equipment: Vauxhall Astra, Vauxhall dealer, driver, OCD, human specimen.

Method: Past experiments have indicated that CBT is gaining strength whereas OCD has been weakening. However, this experiment puts Joe in a vulnerable position. The conditions are perfect for OCD to flourish as Joe is leaving a large object that he has touched many times before and he will never see it again, let alone be able to tap it. Also Joe will be completely enclosed within the car as he is driven to the Vauxhall dealer. However, the experiment will be executed in the morning when Joe will have had a good night's sleep and will not be tired. Both CBT and OCD have been dealt a good hand.

OCD's advantages:

- OCD has control of the whole car.
- Joe is surrounded by the car.
- Joe has been in contact with the car for a long time.
- The car journey is long and will allow anxiety to inflate.

CBT's advantages:

- Joe has been trained in CBT well and can use it effectively.
- Joe is not tired.
- Joe has the help of citalopram.
- Joe has a great deal of willpower wanting to overcome OCD.
- Joe has his family present who can comfort him and reduce anxiety which acts as a catalyst for OCD.

Results: Joe experienced an increase in anxiety and the temptation to perform OCD rituals yet overwhelming willpower helped him to challenge OCD. He was comforted by his family and left the old car at the Vauxhall dealers with no desire to return. He experienced an increase in confidence and willpower.

The next experiment shall be the last and must be the most

extreme and radical experiment performed, so should be well prepared for...

Experiment 3: Defying compulsion

Hypothesis: If a person with OCD can completely defy his illness and eventually return to a healthy anxiety level, the OCD's validity will be destroyed.

Equipment: Human specimen, plastic bottles, OCD, and green recycling bin.

Method: Joe will attempt to recite in his head whilst holding a plastic bottle, 'I sincerely want to give my soul to Satan unless I tap this bottle three times', then place the bottle into a green recycling bin and walk back into his house without tapping the bottle. If the attempt is successful, his anxiety levels should eventually reduce and Joe should feel 'normal'.

OCD logic

Safe ← OCD ← OCD ← OCD ← OCD ← Unsafe

CBT logic

Safe → OCD → OCD → OCD → OCD → Unsafe

This final experiment should prove to Joe that the CBT logic is accurate and should identify the falsity in the OCD logic.

Results: Joe completed the experiment and anxiety levels rose but then eventually decreased as was expected.

So CBT allowed me to try out these experiments and come out actually feeling better. I must point out that these experiments did not happen one after the other. It took about two years to get from the first to the last experiment – two painful years of feeling on edge as I was continually being subjected to these tests. The million-dollar question is, 'Could I have endured the experiments without medication?'. I don't know the answer. The closest that I can give to an answer is that it helped. And, in my opinion and experience citalopram is one of the drugs that might be useful and luckily was the one that worked for me.

However, there are both ethical and physical implications of taking medication.

Is it right to take drugs that can change your mood? And in what ways do these drugs change your mood? The first question I definitely can't answer, and it would be wrong for me to do so. People have different attitudes towards this. I feel that CBT is an ideal way to conquer OCD and depression, as it does not have side effects and is a worthwhile test of willpower; 'that which does not kill me makes me stronger'.

However, when CBT is not working and you feel like you are stuck in quicksand, I found that citalopram can be useful. The second question I cannot answer as a professional but I can promise you that it does not change you in a psychedelic, LSD-style way. All your thoughts are your own and you can still think rationally. When something inconvenienced me, I still got annoyed in the same way that all regularly functioning humans do. If something bad happened it would still upset me. The difference was that I was seeing things in a much clearer context; what I had seen before was a gross caricature of the real world and real human emotions. So the drugs weren't making me less myself but in fact the complete opposite. Depression and OCD were not part of me, Joe: so I was shedding something which had attached itself like a parasite. So if I was still myself, then these drugs weren't immoral; I could still make my own decisions.

So what were the physical implications? It was explained to me before I went on the citalopram that there could be some side effects.

Note to users: this drug could have the following side effects:

- sickness
- dizziness
- baldness
- infertility
- irreversible tentacle growth
- growth of an extra head
- spontaneous combustion
- exploding face syndrome.

Well, not quite that drastic, but when I looked on the back of the packet the side effects looked quite scary. I didn't know which of them would affect me and how badly. I am not a biologist so I can't give you any statistics. I can only tell you that I had one side effect from the drug and that was a slight sickness if I did not eat with them, which was no real problem; I just had to make sure I had breakfast in the morning which was when I took the tablets. Also, it is advised that you should not drink alcohol whilst on the tablets. Obviously I wouldn't know anything about *that*. Well, actually I did find out the hard way that if you drink alcohol at all, even if not to excess, whilst on the tablets, you will start to feel sick. But other than those two things I did not really feel any side effects. Overall, my opinion is that a few side effects are worth it if it helps you stop OCD from ruining your life, however I am not a doctor and anyone should seek medical advice before making a decision about the use of SSRI (selective serotonin reuptake inhibitor) medications.

A small epilogue to my citalopram story. Later on, when I felt comfortable that I had well and truly brought my OCD under control, I decided that it was time to try to come off the citalopram. However, just as you have to be eased onto the drug, you also have to be eased off it. I was on 40 milligrams and the highest dose for an adult (I was told) was 60 milligrams, so 40 milligrams is quite a large dose for a child. At first I wanted to go down to 30 (it's best to go down in tens because any more would be too drastic a drop and I don't think you can get 5 milligram tablets). So, after discussing it with my psychiatrist, I went down to 30 milligrams a day. For the first few days, all was normal, but then gradually my brain began to notice the fact that I had been taking less citalopram and I felt the thoughts just creeping back again. I felt myself getting stressed; I didn't have to act on the thoughts, but they crept back into my mind. At first I thought, 'Right, I'll have to go back up to

40', which a lot of people would do as seems the easiest solution. But then I thought, 'No, I'll stick with this. CBT and willpower have worked before so I'll just have to try it again!'. I used all the various techniques and, after a while, my OCD stabilized and I ended up in the position that I'm in now, where I'm hoping to go down to 20 milligrams. Even though it is important that you keep a close watch on your OCD when you cut medication, and let people know if it creeps back, try not to run off screaming at the first sign of danger. 'Stick with it' because, after all, you don't want to be taking pills all your life if you don't have to.

SUMMARY

» Drugs like citalopram have received a lot of bad press. However, don't take medical advice from the daily tabloid. Ask your doctor or therapist to get the whole picture.

» YOU must make your own judgement on whether to go on the medication and this decision should be based on facts, not hearsay.

» Citalopram is not a 'happy pill' or a 'mind drug'. It does not give you psychedelic hallucinations or come with a free Pink Floyd record.

» This kind of medication is not a cure; you may have to use CBT in conjunction with it.

» Test yourself to see how well you can combat OCD; keep a record or diary.

» If you later want to cut the medication, make sure that you keep an eye on your OCD and tell someone if you have any problems. However, don't retreat up to a higher dosage at the first sign of difficulty. Stick with it; things may improve.

Chapter 15

The Awful Truth

**It takes two to speak the truth –
one to speak and another to hear.**

– HENRY DAVID THOREAU, A WEEK ON THE
CONCORD AND MERRIMACK RIVERS

Until now the only people who knew that I had OCD were Child
and Family Therapy, my direct family and my year head at school.
But my newly found confidence was urging me to tell more people that I had OCD, and to an extent it still does. The subject came
up in a conversation with two friends, and one friend revealed
that her father had OCD. This was the first time I found out that
someone I had met had OCD. I knew that I wasn't the only one
but I'd never met anyone who I actually knew who had it. Until
this moment I had found it intangible that I was not alone with
OCD. So I casually said, 'Oh yeah, I used to have that', but I wasn't
expecting the inquisition that I then received:

'What did you have to do?'

'How bad was it?'

'Do you still have it?'

'Did you have it when I knew you?'

'WOAH!' I said. 'Speak slowly and let me answer.' I spent

about 30 solid minutes explaining pretty much everything, with the exception of one small lie. Even though I had admitted everything else I still did not have the guts to tell them that I still struggled: 'But I don't have it now, I used CBT'. This was about two years ago, probably a few weeks before Experiment 3. OCD was a problem; I could usually handle it, but it was a burden to me that I wanted to get rid of. I could not admit to still being a person with a mental illness; I wanted to be separated from it, an experienced spectator. In fact I had read in Per Hove Thomsen's book *From Thoughts to Obsessions* that only a minority of people who have OCD managed to rid themselves of it completely.

A big change came in admitting to people when Jessica Kingsley Publishers became interested in publishing this book. I was on a school residential trip when I got a call from my mum saying that she'd received an e-mail from them, showing a great deal of interest. I was really pleased and ran down from my dormitory to tell someone. The first person I met was my mate who I had earlier admitted to about my OCD and who had read early manuscripts. She was standing in the doorway to the common room where everybody else was. I told her and another friend who she was talking to, rudely interrupting their conversation, but I had no time for etiquette. I went into the common room and was telling people that I might be getting this book published. They then started asking more questions: the first, 'What's it about?', then 'Ooh what's that?' or, 'Oh I've heard of that'. Then came the big one: 'Do you still have it?'

'Err...', I mumbled, 'well, it never properly goes away but I have control of it now so it doesn't really disrupt my life or stop me from doing stuff.'

'Oh,' they said with a tone of both confusion and acceptance. The questions didn't burrow quite as deep as they had before, perhaps as the fear was not there. 'If he can get a book on it published it's not some weird thing that only he has, he's safe.'

This book talks about parts of the OCD that I would never have dreamed about when my OCD was at its worst. I didn't want to talk about the thoughts, but the more I wrote the more revealing it became, the more light cast on OCD – bringing it out into the open, which is never a bad thing when it comes to OCD. I believe that one reason I was able to get this book into print was because I am one of the first teenagers to talk and write openly about my OCD. OCD is like the bad guy in *Harry Potter*: we don't even want to mention its name. But how on earth are we going to address a problem that has no name, a problem that even our closest friends don't know about? If you're recovering from a leg injury, you want people to know so that they can hold doors open for you and walk at a slower pace if need be. OCD is exactly the same. You need people on your side, an army, loyal friends, who know what to do. It is near impossible to go to war against OCD on your own.

If people had known about my OCD, they would have understood the rituals more and I wouldn't have been under the stress of worrying that people might find out. They could say, 'Are you OK, Joe?', 'D'ya wanna sit down for a moment?', 'We don't mind waiting for you'.

A couple of problems could have arisen from people knowing that I had OCD. The first is that people could have, to put it bluntly, 'taken the mick'. But some people in life are like that and there's little within the law that we can do to stop them. All that you can do is be selective about who you do tell; lots of my friends who I love dearly and who are wonderful people find it hard to keep their mouths shut. Only tell your close friends and make sure they know that this isn't a piece of gossip but something that you 'want them to know', and don't tell people who you feel won't be able to understand it. If you do end up in the situation where someone is having a laugh at your expense all you can do is lean back and feel the warmth of your superiority.

Another problem which may arise is that people can be well-meaning but *too* well-meaning; when some people know that you have OCD but don't understand it properly, a simple act like scratching your nose might to them indicate a relapse and them 'over-worrying' can be irritating to say the least. Don't lose your temper with them. Just tell them that you're OK; they're only concerned about you.

The more that I told people about OCD, the more its compulsions were shown to be a lie, as eventually I felt more and more free from it. There was no exact point when I felt as though it had gone; it just gradually stopped being a problem. I could do anything I wanted – 'the world was my oyster'. I was going out with my friends more, phoning them up and arranging to go places (which I would visit without making rituals). The thoughts popped up now and then but I was in control of them and they seemed to come more out of habit than anything else. I got a Saturday job working at a newsagents, giving people change that I knew that I would never be able to tap. But *now* I had no desire to. It didn't even occur to me. Life was great. 'Where was I before OCD took over about five years ago?'

SUMMARY

» When you tell people that you have OCD they will usually want to know more about it and how you had it.

» Telling people is always helpful. Don't broadcast it to the whole school or office but it's definitely a good idea if a few close friends know.

» Telling people makes it more likely that you'll meet someone else with OCD.

Chapter 16

Getting On with It

Was mich nicht umbringt, macht mich stärker.
(That which does not kill me makes me stronger.)

- FRIEDRICH NIETZSCHE, THE TWILIGHT OF THE IDOLS

I was nine years old the last time I'd felt this free but I didn't appreciate it then. The stress wasn't completely gone, as contrary to popular belief being a teenager isn't easy; I've got GCSE exams soon, I'm writing a book and I'm going out with my mates this weekend. There's so much more that I can do now and I don't even realize. I often go to shows and socialize with my friends; I would have had an OCD-induced heart attack three years ago in the middle of bustling Camden market with only a couple of friends to help, but now I felt fine. I once would have been extremely reluctant to even go in shops, but now I have a job working in one, often on my own; that's a step up. It's often said that OCD seldom goes away completely and that's true, but lots of people may have some worrying thoughts and rituals that do not make them feel uncomfortable and which don't stop them from getting on with their lives. As soon as you are in control of your OCD then you can get on with your life.

It was great that I was feeling better but I felt that I hadn't had 'a life' for five years. I'd hardly ever gone out with friends for *five years*. Five years. So what had I missed? What was the rest of the world doing while I was living the life of a hermit caged in rituals and thoughts?

Well, for a start everyone was 'dating'. Whoops! Bit behind on that one, how embarrassing. There were moral implications to social activities; before it would just be round my house for a tea of fish and chips made by my mum, but now I had to go out places and arrange things myself and decide what I should and shouldn't do. I'd been living half a life since I was nine years old.

Now I was an outsider to OCD, I could explain it better. I was coming from two angles: one, 'This is what I had', and the other, 'This is what it's like for someone with OCD'. I talked to people about OCD and I found that either people had never heard of it, had someone close to them who had it or knew something vague which they'd learnt from a soap opera or from an article in a magazine. The most common symptom that people seem to have heard of is compulsive hand washing; in fact often people believe that OCD is where someone keeps washing their hands and nothing else. It's not ignorance that makes people think this but a lack of information; people with OCD don't want anyone to know in case people don't understand and they don't understand because people with OCD don't talk about it.

Take this scenario as an illustration:

Joe, who has OCD, is frightened that Will might not understand OCD so he doesn't tell Will.

Will, who doesn't have OCD, knows nothing about it except for what he can remember of a magazine article he read.

When Joe vaguely mentions the subject in a conversation, Will reveals his lack of OCD knowledge.

Joe's belief that Will doesn't understand OCD is confirmed but the flawed assumption Joe makes is that this means that Will *can't* understand OCD.

As a result, Joe will never tell Will about OCD and Will keeps his limited knowledge.

So what if the story went a bit more like this:

Joe, who has OCD, is frightened that Will might not understand OCD so he brings it up in a conversation and it turns out that Will knows nothing except for a magazine article he read. So Joe tells Will exactly what it is like. 'How do you know so much?' asks Will and Joe explains that he has OCD. 'Oh, I see,' says Will. 'If you need any help just give me a ring.'

It's much easier if people who can be trusted know that you have OCD. You might want to consider having something like the letter below which you can hand out to people who you know and trust.

Hello

I just wanted to let you know that I have a condition called Obsessive Compulsive Disorder or OCD. It's nothing to panic about. OCD has been around for ages and about 2 in 100 young people have the condition. OCD can come in several forms; the most known is a fear of infection and compulsive hand washing. The different forms can also overlap. At the moment the form of OCD which is affecting me is:

- *fear of dirt and contamination often resulting in obsessive hand washing*
- *counting rituals*
- *need for symmetry or objects to be in just the 'right' position*
- *fear of losing things*
- *hoarding, fear of throwing things out*
- *other*

OCD might cause the things ticked above but it does not make me a different person and will not put you at any risk. This flyer has been given to you to inform you of my current situation. It is also a request for support as I try to change that situation. For more information on OCD try reading From Thoughts to Obsessions or Touch and Go Joe. Or if you are online try going to www.ocdaction.org.uk.

Hope I can rely on your support.

Slightly formal, yes, but the idea is there: people need to know about OCD. There are quite a few silly and uninformed media articles about OCD, and it's up to those who do have OCD to prove how silly these articles are.

In a film screened on TV in 2005, there was a group of people from an OCD support group, *all* of whom seem to have OCD in *all* its forms. Who explained OCD to that writer? Those of us who know about OCD must explain it to others, interrupt other people's conversations, bring it up amongst friends, hand out flyers, if that's what it takes. In Chapter 5 of this book I said that 'OCD appeared to me to be some kind of scandal. I didn't want to talk about it and neither did other people. And if nobody is talking about something then I cannot find out more about it and therefore can't recover from it.' If you tell people about OCD, it will be less of a problem. OCD's effectiveness relies on its secrecy, so think of it as a secret organization – as soon as everyone knows where members meet and what they do, it's no longer the secret organization it used to be.

In my daily life, I feel free from OCD. I still have the thoughts sometimes but they are very much in my subconscious and I rarely notice them. It's as though someone has left the television on in another room and if I listen out I can still hear the faint murmuring of the news headlines. The thoughts never have any effect on me. Sometimes I find myself tapping purely out of habit, but I can stop and it causes me no anxiety. The weight has been lifted from my back. I've made so much progress; there were times when I couldn't walk because of my OCD, yet now I can do whatever I want. So, after five years of struggling from the grasp of OCD, was it worth it?

YEAH!

SUMMARY

» Getting over OCD is hard work and it seldom completely goes away, but when you feel that it is manageable give yourself a big pat on the back – it's not easy!

» Not being controlled by OCD any longer is great; you will be able to get on with your life and all the hard work will be well worth it.

Chapter 17

16 Years Later

In 2004 I began writing this book because my mum told me that if I wrote about my OCD then I could become a millionaire. 16 years later, I realize that she had grossly exaggerated how much money writers earn.

However, after the book was published, I began to tour the country giving talks about my OCD to schools, teacher training events, mental health conferences and anyone else who would have me. At the time having a lecture or workshop lead by a 'service user' (which I find to be quite a clinical term but I haven't come up with a better one yet) was a new and novel idea. I was surprised by how interested the professionals were in my experiences. I guess that OCD is often such a hidden illness, it was unusual for them to get to listen to someone talk so openly about their experiences. The rest of the courses and training events were all about young people's mental health from the outside but I was the only one able to tell them what it was like from the point of view of a young person. It's now fairly standard to have service users involved in training (as well as lots of other aspects of how mental health services work). We're definitely not where we need to be yet but we're heading in an exciting direction.

More and more mental health services are being delivered *with* young people, rather than *to* young people. If you're a young person accessing a mental health service, and you feel confident enough, I would urge you to ask them about opportunities to get involved with shaping how the service works. If there aren't any opportunities then ask them, 'Why not?'

During my OCD talks I would tell some (not very good) jokes and then, when I went to university, I started performing some (slightly better) jokes on the stand-up comedy circuit. Over the years, my jokes got better and comedy is now my main job. Not only have I been fortunate enough to work with some of my favourite comedians, I've also written for topical TV shows and in 2019, even performed on TV myself. I'm so lucky to have been able to turn something I started doing for fun into a living.

I don't think I would be able to do this job if it weren't for the confidence I built up from CBT and overcoming OCD. It can be nerve-racking going onstage at late night comedy clubs where people are drunk and heckling but, having overcome my OCD, I'm now able to do things which would make other people anxious.

I think we undervalue and misunderstand confidence. We don't realize how much of living a happy and successful life is down to having the confidence to decide what you want to be and act on it. We also talk about confidence as though it's an innate thing which you either have or don't have, like being able to roll your tongue, but it isn't. Confidence is something you can learn. CBT helped me learn to be more confident by confronting things which made me anxious. It's a versatile tool which I now use for everything which makes me feel scared or worried.

AVAILABLE FROM ALL GOOD MENTAL HEALTH SERVICES

Since writing this book, a lot of changes have happened in my life. In 2017, I got married to my long-term girlfriend, Danika, whom I met when we were at college. We're both very happy and live in Portsmouth with our two pet guinea pigs (George and Brahms). OCD remains 'not a problem' for me; my measure for this is that there's never a time where I don't do things I want to do or enjoy life fully because of OCD. I haven't needed to take citalopram in over a decade.

Despite all this, I hope that the book doesn't give the impression that I've been 'cured' of obsessive thoughts or that OCD is something which can be cured. I still have to keep on top of it and make sure that it doesn't take on new forms. I sometimes see OCD trying to push its way back in but I'm always one step ahead.

We all have mental health and we all have a responsibility to take care of it, which is something that requires daily maintenance. As we work to ensure that mental health is taken *as seriously* as physical health, I hope that we don't make the mistake of treating it *the same as* physical health. In physical health, generally, if you catch an illness, you can take medicine, then hopefully the illness goes away. With OCD, your thoughts are always there, and worrying is part of being human. It's about making sure that your worries are kept at a manageable level.

I was asked to write an extra chapter for the book, 16 years after writing it. I realized I hadn't even read the book in at least a decade so I thought I ought to reread it. It's all still relevant so I haven't changed much except for a couple of small things like the references to celebrities with OCD. (The original talks about the singer Gabrielle. If you're a teenager reading this then you probably don't know who she is, but her 2001 album *Rise* is on Spotify and totally still holds up.)

When I wrote the book, I hoped that, by telling my story, other OCD sufferers would relate to it and feel less alone. I still get messages and emails from people saying that this has been the case for them. The tips and advice are useful but what is most important about this book is that it is an honest account of my experience with OCD and for that reason, I'm still incredibly proud. Knowing that other people have experienced the same things as you, and that they have overcome the difficulties you are facing, should be an important part of treatment for OCD. Watching the videos on the CD-ROM, which I was given by Alison on my first session, was one of the most important parts of overcoming OCD for me. (One small detail which does date the book is that CD-ROMs don't really exist any more, but they were basically websites which you had to carry around with you.)

Challenging OCD is an immense task, but challenging OCD whilst feeling like you're the only one to have experienced it must be near impossible.

One thing which has changed is that there's a lot more available to read about OCD now; 16 years ago, to find anything written about OCD you had to get a bus to the library and then ask them to order it in from another bigger library then go back a week later to read it. Now, there are loads of books on OCD and they're much easier to get your hands on (so thank you for picking this one). The internet has also meant that anyone can share their experiences and social media gives everyone a platform so that people with OCD from all different backgrounds can be heard.

One of the things I learned after writing the book is that every person with OCD has their own story. Mine was a fairly straightforward story (although it didn't feel straightforward at the time), of someone who got relatively lucky with the circumstances into which they were born. The internet has meant that the stories we can read of people's individual struggles against OCD are more diverse than ever. Social media has opened up a conversation between people with OCD which wasn't there when I had OCD. Any information I give about the online conversation will date quickly, but at the time of writing, Lily Bailey hosts #OCDTalkHour every week on Twitter where people share their experiences and support each other. I hope it's still going in whatever year you are reading this. Other writers like Sarah Collins and Ash Curry share their experiences of OCD on social media and through blogs.

Support for people experiencing OCD from others in the same situation ('peer support' if you want the jargon) has increased in part because the internet has given people the tools to talk to each other, but also because of a huge shift in attitudes to mental health. When I had OCD, people didn't talk about mental illness. The only place it was seen was in horror films, as something to be afraid of, or sometimes in comedy where people with mental illnesses were always the butt of the joke. Now, TV shows like *My Mad Fat Diary* show main characters struggling with their mental health in a way which people can relate to. This is not to say that mental health stigma has gone; it's still a huge problem but things have got so much better than they were, and that proves that things can get even better still.

With all progress there is a backlash and one of the new stereotypes which I hear now about OCD is that it's a 'first world problem', something invented by comfortable middle-class people who have never had to deal with any real adversity so have had to come up with something to make them feel downtrodden. The fact is that OCD can affect anyone from any background and just because some groups have more access to support doesn't mean that OCD is only affecting those groups.

Another piece of news in my life is that at the age of 29 I received an autism diagnosis. I sought it out because my mum told me that whilst I'd been accessing therapy, one of the doctors had recommended that she seek a diagnosis for me. She didn't want me to have another label so didn't take it any further and didn't tell me until I was in my late 20s. Getting the diagnosis changed very little but made a lot of sense. Rereading Chapter 3, it seems so obvious now that I have always been autistic; not liking eye contact, finding it hard to make friends and not liking change. There are also lots of great things about being autistic but that's for another book.

We all have different aspects of who we are and different experiences, some of which we share with others. This book is about my experiences of OCD, something I shared with 2 per cent of the population. I wrote this book for people struggling with OCD (but anyone is free to read it), in the hope that it would be the kind of book which I needed as a teenager, suffering greatly, not knowing what was going on, and feeling like I was the only one.

I hope that it's a substitute for those videos I saw on that CD-ROM. The message I took from those is the most important message in this whole book: that there are other people who are struggling with OCD too, and there are other people who used to struggle with OCD but who (often with a lot of hard work) don't struggle with it any more.

There's a piece of internet slang, TLDR, which stands for 'too long didn't read.' People use it after they've written a long post in a forum so that people who don't want to read the whole thing can get the gist of it even if they don't have all of the details. I'll use it here to summarize this book for anyone who can't be bothered to read the whole thing.

TLDR: You're not on your own, and things can get better.

The 30 › 20 Diary

**Do not take/use citalopram tablets:
If you are allergic to citalopram.**

– LEAFLET IN CITALOPRAM PACKET

This section is for anyone who wants to know more about my experiences of reducing the doses of citalopram. For a long time, right up until the end of my school exams, I was taking precisely 30 milligrams of citalopram every morning. However, once the exam pressure was off I was going to take 20 milligrams of citalopram each day. Below, my diary entries give some idea of my feelings during this period and how it affected me.

Day 1 (Wednesday 22 June)

Thank God that's over. My GCSE exams are out of the way and I think that I did OK, but I won't know till mid-August. This morning I took 30 milligrams of citalopram, hopefully for the last time.

Day 2 (Thursday 23 June)

Got up about half past eight for work at nine, not before taking 20 milligrams of citalopram. I went off to work and spent four boring hours standing at the till whilst virtually nobody came in. The highlight of my day was seeing my friend Lora when she came in to buy beef burgers, so no gripping excitement. I was a bit nervous about reducing my tablets but I knew that it wouldn't take effect for a few days.

Day 3 (Friday 24 June)

Went to work at 9.30 a.m. My boss told me that I would be able to go at one o'clock when he'd take over, so I arrange to go out for lunch with my mum. Half past one, still no sign of him. He says he's out at the bank but he's been gone nearly three hours and he doesn't answer his mobile. Eventually he gets back; I'm not too happy and neither is my mum who's been waiting with me. This really doesn't help my OCD. I'd also told him that I didn't want to work evenings partly because I didn't want to nurture my OCD and partly because I really can't be bothered. Besides the obvious stress related to this incident I haven't felt that the lack of medication has had too much effect on me.

Day 4 (Saturday 25 June)

Went to work for my early morning shift, had a bit of an argument with my boss who tried to get me to work an evening shift, and the end of the story is that I'm only doing my early morning weekend shifts and that means for the next few weeks I'm going to be bored and skint. My mum says she will ask in a local art shop if they need any help. It was also today that I first felt my OCD creeping back; I was in my boss's car and was delivering a paper round with him because one of the paperboys had a hockey tournament. I did not realize it but I felt my hand quickly tapping the door handle as I was about to get out to deliver to number 24. However, when I noticed myself doing it I was able to stop. Was this just coincidence? It's hard to tell but I went back to the shop, picked up the latest *Private Eye* magazine and went home.

Day 5 (Sunday 26 June)

Pretty calm day, no sign of OCD rearing its ugly head. Just stayed at home listening to John Lennon CDs.

Day 6 (Monday 27 June)

Arranged to go out job hunting with Lora, who's also looking for work. I'm deliberating between an art shop in Portsmouth or a stationery store in the nearby town Havant. Went out for a barbeque in the evening and ate way more vegetarian sausages than one man should eat. Even though I was out in the evening I did not feel my OCD creeping back, even when we had an encounter with a group of yobs, who assaulted one of the friends I was walking with for no reason. OCD-wise a very good day.

Day 7 (Tuesday 28 June)

I didn't wake up till 11.30 a.m. Then I tried to eat an 'LP-sized' pizza, bad idea. In the afternoon I went out shopping with my mum. Shopping is an activity which would formerly have seemed like that scene in *Raiders of the Lost Ark* where Indiana Jones dodges numerous traps to reach the Egyptian artefact on top of an elaborate plinth. But today, and recently, shopping has been pretty relaxed and laid back; we just browsed round a few book shops and went home. OCD is nowhere to be seen.

Day 8 (Wednesday 29 June)

One whole week, pretty much OK except for one incident early on when I was about to go out round a friend's house and I found myself performing blinking rituals. 'Hold on a minute,' I thought, 'I don't have to do this any more', and I stopped.

Day 9 (Thursday 30 June)

I'm actually writing this the day after because yesterday was all hustle and bustle. Went to an induction day at my future college, which went pretty well, both for fitting into my college and for OCD. In the evening I went into Brighton to see a band, The Kings Of Leon, with my friend. The crowd was really getting into it and everyone was getting pushed around and I did feel my OCD creeping back. I thought, 'Joe, you don't have to do this', but when I tried to stop the blinking rituals I felt really uncomfortable; just an uneasy feeling like when you have to get your parents to sign a detention slip. I did stop the rituals but I felt uncomfortable about the fact that I felt uncomfortable, and therefore felt more uncomfortable in a kind of vicious circle. But that didn't last too long and I got on with the gig. Still trying to wash beer out of my hair but that's rock 'n' roll!

Day 10 (Friday 1 July)

I went into college with my mum today to look at what support was available for my OCD and they seem quite good there. All my teachers will be aware that I have it and I can talk to a learning support/counsellor person once a week.

Day 11 (Saturday 2 July)

I found myself carrying out some blinking rituals when I woke up to go to work but shook them off quite quickly and the rest of the day was fine.

Day 12 (Sunday 3 July)

Pretty easy day; maybe I've got through all the trouble that I'm going to have.

Day 13 (Monday 4 July)

Went out to Portsmouth with some people that I met at my college induction day. We had a good time, spent hours in the CD sales. OCD was absolutely fine.

Day 14 (Tuesday 5 July)

Still no sign of OCD.

Day 17 (Friday 8 July)

Still no sign. Went back to psychiatrist to discuss how it was going; we told her I was fine.

Day 20 (Monday 11 July)

Well, that was a lot easier than last time I reduced my tablets. There were a few hiccups but I stuck at it and now I feel fine.

Six weeks on 20 milligrams

Well, six weeks later and I'm still fine. After another six weeks I shall be reducing to 10 milligrams and at this rate should be able to come off medication completely by Christmas. I hope this enables you to do the same when the time is right for you. Good luck!

Definition of OCD and CBT

Dr Alison Wallis, Chartered Clinical Psychologist

What is Cognitive Behavioural Therapy (CBT)?

Cognitive Behavioural Therapy is a way of working on problems that uses both the way we think and what we do to help us to start to do things differently and find ways around our problems. To understand CBT it can be can be split into the Cognitive part, the Behavioural part and the Therapy part.

Cognitive means the thinking we do about things. In CBT it means thinking about our thinking and about our behaviour. So when you are working with someone who is trying to help you find solutions to problems in CBT there is a lot of time spent on trying to understand what the thoughts are around the problem, not just what the problem is. Thinking about our thinking is important as our thinking can affect how we feel and what we do.

Behavioural in CBT is about the things that people do.

Therapy means a way of talking about problems that can help to bring about change. In CBT this will mean being more aware of your thinking and of what you do and learning how to think and act differently.

What is Obsessive Compulsive Disorder (OCD)?

Obsessive Compulsive Disorder is when people have thoughts that they don't want and these thoughts make them worry; this worry then leads to behaviours or doing things to try to make the thought go away or to safeguard against it. An example of OCD could be someone who has the thought that they may become ill and who therefore washes their hands over and over again to try to stop this from happening.

Obsessive refers to the intrusive and unwanted thoughts, images, urges, doubts and impulses that occur again and again in the same or similar ways and which cause the worry. These are often distressing and are very hard to ignore.

Compulsive refers to the behaviour associated with the thought. Behaviours are often repeated again and again in response to the thought in an attempt to try to make the thought safe or to stop it from coming true. Compulsions can be physical or mental and often other people have to do compulsions for the person with OCD.

Disorder is when the thoughts and associated behaviours start to become a problem. It may be a problem because it stops someone doing the things that they would like to be able to do or it causes them extreme worry, sometimes also causing people to become very low in mood and tearful.

Some of the patterns of thinking and behaviours associated with OCD can affect us all at some times in our lives. For example, it is common for children to avoid cracks in the pavement in case it makes something bad happen or to wear lucky socks into an exam in the belief that this will improve their marks. If challenged about the belief and the associated behaviour it can be easy to discredit the link; however, people can still feel worried or uncomfortable if they are told not to wear their lucky socks. The rational argument does not always stop the behaviour.

Very often people with OCD are all too aware that the thoughts and the behaviours they use to cope with them do not make sense to others and it can be very hard for people to talk about it. People around them will have tried to reassure them that nothing bad will happen and will have come up with lots of evidence against the thought although this is rarely successful in getting rid of the thought or the behaviour. As such people can often think that they are odd or mad; this along with it being hard to talk about can make meeting a professional like a clinical psychologist very hard and worrying.

How can CBT help with OCD?

CBT links thoughts, feelings and behaviours and tries to change them with the therapist and client working together as a team. When CBT is used for OCD the therapist and client will talk about the thought, the worry that comes from it and the behaviour that the client uses to cope with the thought and the worry. The client is told from the beginning that they will need to stop performing the compulsive behaviour to break the cycle of OCD. It is made clear that they will be helped to do this by learning more about worry and ways to control it and by thinking about their thinking including finding evidence that supports the thought and evidence that could challenge it. They will then be expected to go into situations that cause the obsessive thought and use new skills to help them resist the obsessive thought and compulsive behaviour. The worry often remains that if the compulsive behaviour is not carried out then the thought will come true.

Looking for evidence for this and then against it can help to resist the behaviour. The more often the behaviour is resisted and the thought does not come true, the weaker the thought becomes and the easier it is to resist both the thought and the behaviour.

Working with Joe

Joe had some thoughts that worried him. The biggest and most worrying was that unless he behaved in certain ways he would have his soul stolen. This thought and the worry it gave to Joe had encouraged him to develop a lot of behaviours to try to lessen the chance of him losing his soul.

Joe agreed to work with me and understood the concept of CBT very quickly. We spent some time working on ways in which Joe could control the physical feelings of worry that he experienced but most of our work centred around his thinking. We worked together to find evidence that his soul was going to be taken and evidence against it. Both Joe and I were unsure about how exactly a soul could be taken so we looked for sources that may help us to know under what circumstances others thought that souls could be stolen. For this we looked towards the Bible and asked for help from a chaplain and Joe used the internet. We could find no reports from these sources that souls were just taken. As such we began to think that most people thought that souls would be taken if this was asked for in exchange for something. This seemed to be the most consistent explanation and offered Joe enough evidence against his thought that he was able to begin to resist responding to it with the behaviours he had been using. Once Joe was able to have the thought and not respond to it he was able to start to gather clearer evidence that the behaviours he had been using were not linked to his thought and did not protect him. At this point the thought began to lose its power over Joe and he began to take control of his OCD. Joe and I continued to work together while he tackled situations where the thought had been stronger, and as he made more and more progress he took increasing control of the work.

I understand from Joe and his mum that he continues to use the strategies that we practised together if he notices that OCD is becoming stronger again and that he has continued to make excellent progress.

Bibliography

Beck, A.T. (1976) *Cognitive Therapy and the Emotional Disorders.* New York: International Universities Press.

Salkovskis, P.M. and Kirk, J. (1989) 'Obsessional disorders.' In K. Hawton, P.M. Salkovskis, J. Kirk, and D.M. Clark (eds) *Cognitive Behaviour Therapy for Psychiatric Problems: A Practical Guide.* Oxford: Oxford University Press, pp. 129–68.

World Health Organization (1993) *The ICD 10 Classification of Mental and Behavioural Disorders: Clinical Descriptions and Diagnostic Guidelines.* Geneva: World Health Organization.

OCD Tips and Advice

Worrying

» Everybody has some irrational obsessions like checking twice that they've locked the door, or being a bit fussy with sell-by dates, but it's when these things get in the way of your normal life and are distressing for you that you might have OCD.

» OCD is very hard to explain to people who don't have OCD.

» OCD can gain power over you. When you try not to think about your obsession you can't take your mind off it.

» OCD is not rare; in fact up to two per cent of the population are affected by it in some way.

Poisoning of the mind

» Some people who have OCD become obsessed with avoiding infection and germs (known as 'fear of contamination').

» Of course you should keep yourself clean, and try to stay healthy, but you must always be sensible about what precautions you take to avoid germs.

» If you know that you have these worries try to take 'health warnings' with a pinch of salt. Stay calm.

» If half your brain says, 'Come on, you don't need to keep washing your hands', listen to that half, not the half saying, 'You had better wash your hands again because you touched the door handle on the way out of the bathroom'.

» Germs are inescapable, so apart from taking the precautions that everyone else does, e.g. washing your hands after you go to the loo, don't worry about them.

Only human

» Even if you do have OCD, you are still a person with a name, along with likes, dislikes, talents, shortcomings, etc. Nothing can take that from you.

» OCD can be triggered or made worse by stressful situations, like moving house, starting a new school, or a friend or family member dying.

» You can find something (legal) which you find calming, like a certain type of book, music or art that you like, and exploit its calming effect to its full potential.

» Doing something artistic also helps to calm you down when OCD is strong.

Guilty mind

» The church and religion in general can be a challenge to someone with OCD – the things to remember are to always think for yourself and be sensible.

» Don't worry about what you do in your head. In this world it's what you do and say and how you behave that matters, not what thoughts you have.
» It's helpful to question everything that you are told, even things that you tell yourself.

Am I going mad?

» OCD is not the experience of 'hearing voices'.
» People won't always understand when someone tries to explain OCD to them. My mistake was not explaining it clearly enough – it's best to be as clear as possible when talking about it.
» Don't expect your GP to know much about OCD. GPs are *general* practitioners but should be able to refer you on to someone who specializes in illnesses like OCD.
» Don't let bad experiences put you off telling people that you have OCD: you are much better off with it out in the open.

Learning to count

» OCD can change from one form to another.
» Some people with OCD become obsessed with counting or doing certain things a certain number of times, or in a certain way.
» These numbers or number sequences may gradually get bigger and bigger, becoming more unmanageable.
» Irrational compulsions like this are referred to as 'rituals'.

- » It is hard to keep these things a secret from people.
- » The numbers or number sequences are often triggered by thoughts that something bad will happen if the ritual is not carried out.
- » These thoughts can be challenged by thinking to yourself, 'Nothing bad will happen whether I do this ritual or not!'.

Keeping my secret

- » You will find lots of ways to try to hide OCD as it may seem embarrassing or weird.
- » Hiding OCD is actually counterproductive.

Learning to walk the walk

- » Sometimes OCD may make you walk a certain way or count the steps that you walk.

OCD abroad

- » The people who care about you will struggle themselves, having to watch you struggle.
- » Give your parents feedback on what helps you and what doesn't. They're only human and probably don't know what it's like, so guide them.
- » Be aware of holidays. OCD can thrive in unfamiliar situations. However, this doesn't mean that you should avoid them; just be prepared.

Getting help

» Get your GP to refer you on to a therapist or someone else who can help you.

» Modern therapists are not like they are on TV; it's much more relaxed and nothing to worry about.

» Don't be embarrassed to tell these specialists about the things that OCD makes you think or do; they will have heard similar things before.

» Having help with combating OCD does help a lot! It can feel virtually impossible to overcome OCD on your own.

» A therapist is not the same as other doctors; you have to help yourself too. There is no miracle pill that cures you on its own.

Convincing myself of OCD's irrationality

» OCD is a very silly illness: the things that it makes you do make no sense but to someone who has OCD they seem to make a lot of sense.

» It is hard to convince someone with OCD that it is silly but an expert can teach a person how to be more rational.

Challenging

» Cognitive Behavioural Therapy (CBT) is used to treat OCD. CBT helps you change your behaviour so that it is based on solid facts and sound logic.

» You can use this sound logic and solid facts to challenge the OCD thoughts.

» Therapists can train you in CBT, but it's up to you to use it.

» You can measure your anxiety from one to ten using a gauge; this helps to show other people how you are feeling.

Depression and OCD

» OCD can really get you down, so collaborates well with depression as when you feel down OCD gets worse and vice versa.

» Depression is more than just having a bad day; it can really affect your life.

» Lots of teenagers may feel down because of hormones and this can be part of adolescence.

» If depression is, in your opinion, becoming a problem and inflaming OCD you should tell someone, preferably a therapist if you are seeing one.

Citalopram

» Drugs like citalopram have received a lot of bad press. However, don't take medical advice from the daily tabloid. Ask your doctor or therapist to get the whole picture.

» YOU must make your own judgement on whether to go on the medication and this decision should be based on facts, not hearsay.

» Citalopram is not a 'happy pill' or a 'mind drug'. It does not give you psychedelic hallucinations or come with a free Pink Floyd record.

» This kind of medication is not a cure; you may have to use CBT in conjunction with it.

» Test yourself to see how well you can combat OCD; keep a record or diary.

» If you later want to cut the medication, make sure that you keep an eye on your OCD and tell someone if you have any problems. However, don't retreat up to a higher dosage at the first sign of difficulty. Stick with it; things may improve.

The awful truth

» When you tell people that you have OCD they will usually want to know more about it and how you had it.

» Telling people is always helpful. Don't broadcast it to the whole school or office but it's definitely a good idea if a few close friends know.

» Telling people makes it more likely that you'll meet someone else with OCD.

Getting on with it

» Getting over OCD is hard work and it seldom completely goes away, but when you feel that it is manageable give yourself a big pat on the back – it's not easy!

» Not being controlled by OCD any longer is great; you will be able to get on with your life and all the hard work will be well worth it.

Further Information

When OCD appears in the media – which is a rarity – it either appears as tabloid-esque drivel designed to get people's attention and to fuel ideas to hypochondriacs, or as items packed full of scientific jargon and seemingly irrelevant statistics. Whilst writing this book, I sieved through everything that I could get my hands·on, about or around the subject of OCD, and found a few gems, which might be useful. Here's a list of a few resources that I recommend to you.

Can I Tell You about OCD?: A Guide for Friends, Family and Professionals (2013) by Amita Jassi, published by Jessica Kingsley Publishers, London.

This book follows Katie, a 13-year-old with OCD who is going through CBT. It's a short book which is really easy to read but it's packed full of useful advice for young people with OCD. It would also be useful for teachers and family members to get a brief introduction to OCD.

The Consolations of Philosophy (2001) (Chapter 1) by Alain De Botton, published by Penguin Books, London.

I have included this book because it explores different problems which we all face such as: unpopularity, frustration, inadequacy, a broken heart, and so on. De Botton explores these problems and the first chapter on unpopularity is also a very useful device when practising CBT as it is so heavily embedded in logic and reason.

Breaking Free From OCD: A CBT Guide for Young People and Their Families (2008) by Jo Derisley, Isobel Heyman, Sarah Robinson and Cynthia Turner, published by Jessica Kingsley Publishers, London.

Written like a school workbook with exercises to be filled in, this book uses CBT techniques and talks about the thought processes which lead to the beliefs that we have. It then gives you a way to reach more accurate and helpful beliefs. The book encourages readers to write down their thoughts, something which I found useful when I was going through CBT.

From Thoughts To Obsessions (1999) by Per Hove Thomsen, published by Jessica Kingsley Publishers, London.

This is a very factual book and contains lots of research and statistics about OCD, its causes, characteristics and treatments. It has a few case studies which also helped me to realize that I was not alone in having OCD. My mum said she found this book very useful, because it was the first source of information that she had read on OCD, and it set her mind at rest that OCD was not related to psychotic mental illness such as schizophrenia. It also showed that OCD was not related to parenting style or family functioning, which was comforting for her as parents often feel they are to blame or that others will blame them if their children have difficulties.

OCD-UK (www.ocduk.org)

> An organization set up to help people with OCD. This website is a good way to interact with other people affected by OCD (without the intimidation of actually meeting people) through social media and discussion forums. They also run some support groups.

The Secret Problem (1994) by Chris Wever, with drawings by Neil Phillips, published by Shrink-Rap Press, Concord West, NSW.

> A very brief illustrated introduction to OCD for children, teenagers and their parents, although the 'OCD-opus' octopus character will be more popular among younger children. At times though, the book sometimes risks making OCD look simple to overcome. This book can be ordered from www.shrinkrap.com.au.

Passing for Normal: A Memoir of Compulsion (2000) by Amy Wilensky, published by Scribner, London.

> Amy has had OCD since she was eight years old and the book focuses on her struggle to cover it up and 'pass for normal'. Entertaining and informative at the same time.

Obsessive Compulsive Disorder Diary: A Self-Help Diary with CBT Activities to Challenge Your OCD (2020) by Charlotte Dennis, published by Jessica Kingsley Publishers, London.

> This book is unlike any other book I've read about OCD, it's part diary and part CBT workbook. Whilst you complete the CBT activities you can also see how Charlotte has completed them herself which is a great way of making the reader feel that they aren't alone.

Stand Up to OCD!: A CBT Self-Help Guide and Workbook for Teens (2019) by Kelly Wood and Douglas Fletcher, published by Jessica Kingsley Publishers, London.

Stand up to OCD starts out like a graphic novel where OCD is represented as a sort of goblin creature, ruining young people's lives with intrusive thoughts. It goes on to become a workbook with CBT activities for you to complete.

Index